PICASSO

GRAPHIC MAGICIAN

The catalogue accompanies the exhibition held at:

Iris & B. Gerald Cantor Center
for Visual Arts at Stanford University
January 24 – March 28, 1999

Toledo Museum of Art
November 7, 1999 – January 16, 2000

Norton Simon Museum
April 13 – June 18, 2000

The exhibition was made possible
by a generous gift from John and
Jill Freidenrich

ILLUSTRATIONS
Dust jacket/Front cover
**Bacchanal with Young Goat and
Onlooker** (detail) (cat. 47)

Half-title page
**Marie-Thérèse as a Woman
Bullfighter** (cat. 8.14)

Title page 3
The Pipers (cat. 20.2)

First published in 1998 by
Philip Wilson Publishers Limited
143-149 Great Portland Street
London W1N 5FB

in association with
Iris & B. Gerald Cantor Center for
Visual Arts at Stanford University

Distributed in the USA and Canada by
Antique Collectors' Club
Market Street Industrial Park
Wappingers' Falls
New York 12590
USA

ISBN 0-937031-13-5 paper
      0-85667 494 X hard
Library of Congress Catalog Card
Number 98-61086

Edited by Cherry Lewis
Designed by Sara Robin

Printed and bound in Italy by
Società Editoriale Libraria per azioni,
Trieste

As many of our illustrated books have had pages removed, or pictures cut out we are now monitoring such books. Please fill in the following to indicate that this book was still complete when you returned it.

Name	Signature	Date Returned	Checked By

PICASSO

GRAPHIC MAGICIAN

PRINTS FROM THE NORTON SIMON MUSEUM

BETSY G. FRYBERGER

GLORIA WILLIAMS

CLINTON ADAMS

DAVID CARRIER

PAT GILMOUR

IRIS & B. GERALD CANTOR CENTER
FOR VISUAL ARTS AT STANFORD UNIVERSITY
IN ASSOCIATION WITH PHILIP WILSON PUBLISHERS

CONTENTS

FOREWORDS

THOMAS K. SELIGMAN 7

SARA CAMPBELL 9

PICASSO:
GRAPHIC MAGICIAN
PRINTS FROM THE
NORTON SIMON MUSEUM

BETSY G. FRYBERGER 10

NORTON SIMON:
COLLECTING AND THE
TASTE FOR PICASSO

GLORIA WILLIAMS 26

PICASSO'S
LITHOGRAPHS,
1945–1949

CLINTON ADAMS 40

MARIE-THERESE:
A PERFECT ODALISQUE

PAT GILMOUR 56

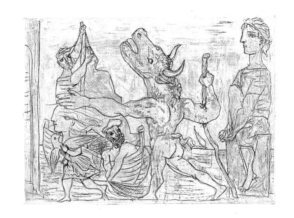

PAINTING AS
PERFORMANCE ART:

THE CASE OF PICASSO

DAVID CARRIER 74

CATALOGUE OF
THE EXHIBITION

BETSY G. FRYBERGER 114

APPENDIX

CHECKLIST OF THE
NORTON SIMON
MUSEUM COLLECTIONS

166

NOTES

171

BIBLIOGRAPHY

174

WOMAN WITH FLOWERED BLOUSE (cat. 41)
December 27, 1958
Lithograph, worked with wash and engraving needle, on zinc

FOREWORD

THOMAS K. SELIGMAN
JOHN AND JILL FREIDENRICH DIRECTOR
IRIS & B. GERALD CANTOR CENTER
FOR VISUAL ARTS AT STANFORD UNIVERSITY

Celebrating the accomplishment of a supremely innovative artist, *Picasso: Graphic Magician* is a fitting opening exhibition for the Iris & B. Gerald Cantor Center for Visual Arts at Stanford University. This new center signals a renewed commitment to building an important modern and contemporary art program, and to presenting exhibitions with strong ties to the University's teaching program. I believe this exhibition and catalogue reflect what good museum collaborations are all about—creativity, mutual support, and an intense desire to share with the public the treasures and knowledge we have. I hope this effort will set the stage for future collaborations between the Norton Simon Museum and Stanford.

I first met Norton Simon and Sara Campbell, who was then curator of his private collection and foundation, in the early 1970s. At the time I was at the Fine Arts Museums of San Francisco, where we benefited from a number of loans of French painting and sculpture to the Legion of Honor and several major European paintings to the de Young. I learned of Mr. Simon's serious interest in higher education as we developed programs around these loans, relying on the advice of scholars at the University of California, Berkeley and at my alma mater, Stanford University. When I returned to Stanford in 1991, it seemed entirely fitting to renew my contact with Sara Campbell, now director of art at the Norton Simon Museum. Our chief curator, Bernard Barryte, initiated the idea for this exhibition with Norton Simon curator Gloria Williams in 1995 and has been very helpful in its subsequent development. Recognizing that it was twenty-five years since the death of Picasso, it seemed an appropriate time for a reassessment of his printmaking achievements.

Picasso: Graphic Magician has been organized by Betsy G. Fryberger, our curator of prints and drawings, working with Gloria Williams; they have been ably assisted by the staff at both museums. At Stanford, Letitia Yang assisted in the catalogue preparation, as have Arlene Gray, Leslie Johnston, Kerry Morgan, Jill Osaka, and Minoti Pakrasi; Noreen Ong has made the loan arrangements. At the Norton Simon Museum, Gloria Williams's research was aided by Sara

Campbell's recollections, conversations with Robert Light, and correspondence with Heinz Berggruen. Registrar Andrea Clark, Jennifer Zapanta, Sharon Goodman, and Bethany Spenceman assisted in cataloguing the comprehensive Picasso print collection.

This catalogue makes a valuable addition to the enormous body of scholarship devoted to Picasso. We are grateful to the authors, Clinton Adams, David Carrier, Betsy G. Fryberger, Pat Gilmour, and Gloria Williams. Our thanks to Carol M. Osborne and Fronia W. Simpson for editorial consultation. We welcome the opportunity to publish this handsome scholarly catalogue jointly with Philip Wilson Publishers, Ltd.

John and Jill Freidenrich, who had already done so very much to help us rebuild the damaged Stanford Museum, provided the funding that has made the exhibition and catalogue possible. Their relationship to the Simon family goes back many years, and when they learned of our plans for this exhibition, they once again came forward with generous support.

I am especially grateful to Sara Campbell, the trustees of the Norton Simon Museum and Foundation, and Jennifer Jones Simon for generously agreeing to these loans.

FOREWORD

SARA CAMPBELL
DIRECTOR OF ART
NORTON SIMON MUSEUM

*P*icasso: *Graphic Magician* provides an occasion to consider the extraordinary spectrum of Picasso's creative efforts as a printmaker. This review is facilitated by the quality and scope of the Picasso prints that were acquired by Norton Simon, while the exhibition affords a unique opportunity to explore Norton Simon's well-known affection for Picasso as a graphic artist. Less well known is Norton Simon's commitment to higher education and the role of university art galleries in campus life.

During the early 1970s, Simon's "museum without walls" program lent major portions of his collections to many college and university art galleries. Students throughout the country benefited, as the collections traveled to Harvard, Oberlin, Princeton, Pomona, Smith, Wellesley, Yale, the University of Washington, and the University of California campuses at Los Angeles, Berkeley, Irvine, and Riverside. When in 1974 the collections moved to their new home in Pasadena, the lending program ended. A significant exception was the loan of a monumental Barbara Hepworth sculpture to Stanford University to celebrate the opening of the new Stanford Law School building in 1975.

Now, to commemorate another successful Stanford building program, the establishment of the Iris & B. Gerald Cantor Center for Visual Arts, we continue the tradition of Norton Simon's support of the important place of art in higher education. The Norton Simon Museum is privileged to participate in this inaugural exhibition.

FIGURE 1

MODEL AND SCULPTOR WITH HIS SCULPTURE (cat. 8.4)
March 17, 1933
Etching
From *Suite Vollard*, plate 38

PICASSO: GRAPHIC MAGICIAN
PRINTS FROM THE NORTON SIMON MUSEUM

BETSY G. FRYBERGER
CURATOR OF PRINTS AND DRAWINGS
IRIS & B. GERALD CANTOR CENTER
FOR VISUAL ARTS AT STANFORD UNIVERSITY

Picasso's many faces continue to fascinate, twenty-five years after his death. New scholarship has increasingly documented the highly autobiographical content of his work and his enduring dialogue with old masters of European art and with his Spanish heritage.

To select and thus confine his enormous oeuvre within the framework of any single exhibition is challenging, whether the focus is on a single chronological period or on one medium —painting, sculpture, drawing, or printmaking—each facet revealing only part of his formidable achievements. The Museum of Modern Art in New York has long been a leader in organizing comprehensive retrospectives of his painting and sculpture, and most recently of his portraiture.[1] Two recent exhibitions of prints from the family collections have featured rarely seen trial proofs and monotypes, which offer unusually intimate and technically innovative windows on his work. One, which toured in this country, was based on the Marina Picasso collection; the other, on holdings in the Musée Picasso in Paris. Both catalogues were written by Brigitte Baer, who in brilliantly mining the wealth of Picasso's printmaking has deepened our understanding.[2]

The essays presented in this exhibition catalogue document diverse aspects of his printmaking. My introductory remarks focus on the 120 prints selected from the Norton Simon Museum's impressive holdings and their place in the evolution of Picasso's printmaking. Gloria Williams, curator at the Norton Simon Museum, details in her essay Simon's collecting philosophy and his practical priorities, which explain why the Museum has so many works as sets and proofs in series. Professor Clinton Adams, a distinguished practitioner and teacher of lithography for many years at the University of New Mexico, brings his technical expertise to illuminate Picasso's engagement with that medium. Pat Gilmour, who has written extensively on 20th-century printmaking, explores the history of Picasso's relation to his mistress Marie-Thérèse Walter as revealed in his prints. Finally, Professor David Carrier, who teaches philosophy at Carnegie-Mellon University and contributes stimulating articles on many aspects of art in a broad cultural context, examines Picasso's attraction to performance and his role as performer.

Picasso: Graphic Magician focuses on four major phases of Picasso's printmaking, each distinctive in choice of subject as well as technical handling. The first group is composed of etchings dating from the 1930s. Included are illustrations to classic texts by Ovid and Balzac and the major *Suite Vollard*, in which scenes of a sculptor in his studio are the dominant motif, but close to the end a Minotaur enters the arena and the imagery grows darker. The etchings of the early years in the decade are characterized by a cool but distant mastery of line and later by a heightened emotionality matched by more subtle and complex technical effects.

The lithographs of the late 1940s printed at the workshop of Fernand Mourlot in Paris form the second clearly defined group in which Picasso, through unconventional means, redefines naturalistic subjects, paring them down to minimalist abstractions. Again technical manipulation of conventional tools combined with unorthodox ones (an engraving needle) play an integral role in achieving the astonishing images. Among the most complex subjects are several after paintings by Cranach and Delacroix, in which Picasso challenges and reinvents tradition. Portraiture is a significant late component of this period, with images of Françoise Gilot followed by those of Jacqueline Roque.

The third group, the linocuts of the late 1950s and early 1960s, reveals Picasso again devising an ingenious approach. Instead of doing the expected, he reused the same block with repeated recarving. Among his most exuberant prints are scenes of bullfights and bacchanals, which alternate with large decorative heads.

In marked contrast to the oversize and public nature of the linocuts, Picasso's last chapter of printmaking closes with private concerns and obsessions. Still inventive technically, with the assistance of the Crommelynck brothers, these late etchings, which include *Suite 347* of 1968, are direct and deeply experienced, without artifice. Irony and ribald humor, seldom self-pity, characterize Picasso's reflections on his failing powers and his place in history.

Picasso confided to his longtime art dealer Daniel-Henry Kahnweiler that he thought of printmaking as a disguise, because the plate or block was cut or carved in reverse, thereby obscuring the image, which appears only after being printed on a sheet of paper.[3] To understand Picasso's work one has to penetrate the artist's disguises, for his prodigious inventiveness hides as well as reveals. In his art, as in his life, Picasso played many roles: as an innovator of new modes of transcribing (Cubism and Surrealism); as an artist conversant with the European tradition of painting, exemplified in works by Rembrandt as well as by such French precursors as Delacroix, Manet, and Cézanne; and as artistic heir to Spanish masters from El Greco and Velázquez to Goya. In conversations with Matisse, Picasso spoke of his work in the large context of history.[4] However, European masters constituted only one catalyst. African carvings and "fetishes", Cycladic sculpture, postcards, magazines, newspapers, even television nourished his creativity. His personal collection of ephemera and photography included 19th-century portraits, snapshots of friends, and African tribal dress.[5] Life itself sustained his omnivorous appetite.

For over sixty years Picasso experimented in printmaking's range of techniques. He was, like Degas, primarily a painter and sculptor, who made prints only sporadically. When each made prints, drawing from his mental inventiveness and openness to use unorthodox tools and techniques, each achieved highly individualistic and original results. Each artist found in monotype the painter's private print medium.

Trying to trace and reconstruct Picasso's artistic journey involves detours and at times the trail divides, leading simultaneously into channels as dissimilar as Surrealism and Neo-classicism as, for example, in the *Suite Vollard* etchings (cat. 8). His printmaking appears to come close to full circle, when in 1968 he returned to circus scenes in *Suite 347* (cat. 53) seemingly similar to those of his Blue Period (cat. 1). However, where in the early images an acrobat is observed by an outsider, in those drawn sixty years later the narrator is an almost constant player and the scenes are more complex and layered. David Carrier in his essay explicates these issues of performance. Picasso's love of the circus is recounted by his friend the photographer Brassaï, who often joined him in the audience at the Cirque Médrano.[6] Brassaï noted that although Picasso was drawn to clowns and their role-playing, he rarely attended theater performances.

Early and late in his career, Picasso often adopted the circus as his stage, but during the 1930s in the *Suite Vollard*, the artist's studio moves to center stage, where artist and muse act out different roles—the artist as classical god, the muse as mistress. By 1968 Picasso's cast is highly autobiographical, a parade of mistresses and wives, parents and friends, who consort with or have been transformed into dancers and circus performers. Alternating with personal recollections are encounters with great artists, resulting in variations and parodies of artists from El Greco to Ingres. In this web of memory and fantasy, two sustaining threads often merge—love and sex, and the act of artistic creation. Picasso's voracious appetite for life continues, but often he shows himself as an old fool or a voyeur, surrounded by or spying on beautiful youth.

Images of the circus (cats. 1.1–1.2) initiate Picasso's printmaking activity and introduce the exhibition. However, within only a few years his prints were directed elsewhere, to furthering his experiments with Cubism in which formal rather than figurative motifs predominate. Several compositions were published in book form, accompanying texts of his friend the poet Max Jacob (cat. 2). These illustrations and the single large etching *Still Life with Bottle of Marc* (cat. 4) were published by Kahnweiler, who also published Braque's equally famous Cubist print *Fox*.

ETCHINGS OF THE 1930S

Only in the 1930s, when Picasso was in his fifties, did he complete a substantial and coherent body of printed work, mainly in the form of etchings commissioned and published by Ambroise Vollard, the Parisian dealer whose enthusiasm for prints was crucial to the creation of the *livre d'artiste*, a new book form in which original prints supplanted the text in primacy of importance.

Two of Picasso's most important illustrated books were published in 1931. Vollard commissioned illustrations for Balzac's *Chef-d'oeuvre inconnu*, the story of an obsessive and reclusive artist (cat. 5). The young Swiss Albert Skira began his publishing career with the commission of the second book, Ovid's *Métamorphoses*, a collection of tales of adventures and loves of gods and goddesses (cat. 6). The major print publication was the hundred etchings in the *Suite Vollard* (cat. 8). Its longest sequence centers on the artist in the studio, but transposes Balzac's subject into a setting in which gods, centaurs, and nymphs enter the studio, where they encounter a handsome, bearded artist and his muse/model/mistress. The artist is both godlike and like Picasso's own bearded father (fig. 1). The models and mistresses include likenesses of Marie-Thérèse Walter, Sarah (wife of the painter Gerald) Murphy, and a dark-haired model who closely resembles Françoise Gilot (whom Picasso had not yet met, but whose type of dark beauty and strong features he admired).[7] Many studio scenes include a large sculpted bust of his current mistress, Marie-Thérèse, on which Picasso was then at work in his studio at Boisgeloup, outside Paris. Brassaï, whose sensitive eye Picasso trusted, took haunting photographs of these monumental plasters.[8]

Marie-Thérèse's many appearances in the *Suite Vollard* etchings are noted by Gilmour in her essay. In scenes dating from later in the decade, a Minotaur enters the narrative, first participating in a friendly bacchanal, but when he takes on the sculptor's role, violence and rape follow. Michel Leiris has commented on the human qualities of Picasso's Minotaur, noting a family likeness between it and the bearded sculptor, in contrast to André Breton's official Surrealist interpretation of the beast as a symbol of the unconscious.[9] Among the final plates in the *Suite Vollard* are three depictions of a blind Minotaur (cats. 8.15–8.17) whose erect body is clearly human, but surmounted by a head of a bull (fig. 2). The imagery in the *Suite Vollard* plates grew more complex at the same time that Picasso began working with a new printer, Roger Lacourière, in 1936. As he became more engaged in understanding tonal intaglio techniques, Picasso experimented with sugar-lift aquatint, which permits areas of wash to be brushed or painted directly on the plate (in much the same way a line can be drawn into the ground of a copperplate and later etched). Instead of continuing to use etching primarily as a vehicle to reproduce his line drawings, Picasso varied the biting of the plate and built up layers of wash. These technical subtleties give depth to the characterization of the blind Minotaur.

Some of Picasso's most lighthearted etchings and aquatints were published as illustrations for the 18th-century classic *Histoire naturelle* by the comte de Buffon (cat. 11). The thirty animals—from a stomping bull to a crayfish—were drawn rapidly, with the artist completing a print each day for a month, collaborating with the printer Lacourière. This book, the last Vollard commissioned from Picasso, remained unpublished at the time of Vollard's death in 1939, one of his many unfinished projects.

After Picasso visited Spain in the late summer of 1934, the bullfight became the disturbingly violent theme of two large etchings in which Marie-Thérèse is shown stretched across the back of a gored horse (cats. 9 and 10). The imagery of his monumental *Minotauromachia* etching of the following year is linked to other earlier images, including these two scenes as well as several plates of the *Suite Vollard* (cats. 8.15–8.17, 8.19). These etchings prefigure passages in Picasso's *Guernica* (Museo Nacional Centro de Arte Reina Sofía, Madrid), titled in remembrance of the bombing of the Basque city by Franco's German allies in April 1936. Picasso painted this monumental mural in Paris in a new studio on the rue des Grands-Augustins (the setting of Balzac's *Chef-d'oeuvre inconnu*, an association he relished). Several of the *Guernica* images—the weeping woman, the woman with dead child, and the Minotaur—appear in the small but passionately felt anti-Franco caricatures (cat. 12).[10]

During the turbulent years preceding and continuing through the Second World War, Picasso made few prints. His friend Max Jacob died in a concentration camp in 1944; the following spring his mistress Dora Maar became seriously ill.

FIGURE 2
**BLIND MINOTAUR GUIDED BY MARIE-THERESE
WITH PIGEON ON A STARRY NIGHT** (cat. 8.17)
December 1934–January 1935
Aquatint, scraper, drypoint, and burin
From *Suite Vollard*, plate 97

FIGURE 3
**WOMAN IN AN ARMCHAIR, NO. 4
(FROM THE VIOLET ZINC PLATE)** (cat. 26)
December 10, 1948–January 3, 1949
Lithograph in wash on zinc

LITHOGRAPHS OF THE 1940S AND 1950S

Picasso had tried lithography in the 1920s, with a halting and surprisingly clumsy touch (far removed from the elegant Ingresque pencil drawings of a few years earlier), and, during the 1930s when he was actively etching, he made no lithographs. Only in late 1945 and early 1946 at Mourlot's workshop did Picasso become fully engaged. This second major phase of Picasso's printmaking is analyzed by Clinton Adams in his essay. Adams emphasizes, as have Baer and Gilmour, that only when Picasso worked directly and closely with a printer did he attain his most brilliant and innovative prints.[11]

Activities in the Mourlot workshop have been described by Gilot, the young painter who was at that time Picasso's lover.[12] Although she posed for paintings and drawings, she played a relatively minor role in the winter's first lithographs. In *Two Nude Women* (cat. 14) her features can be recognized in the face of the seated woman, as can those of Picasso's former mistress, Dora Maar, in the sleeping woman. When on June 14 Gilot became the focus of his attention, Picasso made not one but ten crayon sketches of her face that were transferred to stone (Mourlot 38–47).[13] The rapidly taken likenesses were at first naturalistic, emphasizing her large eyes, long lashes, pointed eyebrows, straight nose, and her face framed by a mass of hair. In the process of abstraction, her head became the center of a circle of rays of light or flower petals, as a sun- or flower-woman (Mourlot 48). To emphasize her independence, Picasso painted her standing (most portrayals of other mistresses show them seated or lying down). In 1948 Gilot dressed in a Polish coat was the subject of a composition intended to be printed in five colors—an experiment unusual for Picasso in its use of color and one that failed (Mourlot 133). He did not, however, abandon the five zinc plates; rather, he reworked each and had each printed in black (fig. 3). These variants are among his boldest and most radical lithographs, yet they were executed with subtle tonal detail (Mourlot 134–38).[14] In April 1949 he created two hieratic Egyptian stylizations of Gilot, one with green hair (cat. 37), a second with a striped bodice (Mourlot 179).[15]

When Picasso began to spend more time in the Midi, painting and making ceramics, the Mourlot workshop in Paris became too distant. Aside from some book illustrations and posters, he made few lithographs, and many of them are transfers. Among the most ambitious and fully finished are several portraits of women. In *Françoise against a Gray Background* Picasso portrayed her in a pensive mood (cat. 31). Three years later, in 1953, by then the mother of his son Claude and daughter Paloma, she is seen reading in a rare domestic scene with her small children in *Games and Reading* (cat. 33), but within the year she had left Picasso.[16]

A new direction in Picasso's lithography resulted from his interest in paintings by Cranach and Delacroix. Attracted to the 16th-century German painter's strangely elongated women, Picasso adapted several subjects, among them David and Bathsheba (cats. 23 and 24), Venus and Cupid, and a portrait of a noblewoman (cat. 42).[17] In his revision of David and Bathsheba he did not bother to reverse the composition (necessary if the subject were to appear in the same direction as the painting when printed). In rephrasing the composition, Picasso undoubtedly saw himself as the king—powerful but aging—watching the youthful women (Gilot). Bathsheba and her tall companion wear distinctive leaflike headdresses similar to the leaves in the sun- or flower-woman paintings with which Picasso framed Gilot's head. The simplified leaf silhouettes recall Matisse's cutouts, which Picasso and Gilot had seen on their visits and of which Picasso took note. Although work on the lithograph began in 1947, the print had an interrupted gestation.[18]

Picasso presented several paintings to the French government in 1946 and had the opportunity of privately seeing his work in the Louvre, placed first in the French galleries, then in the Spanish. Gilot has described Picasso's elation at how well his work looked with the old masters and how he returned repeatedly to study Delacroix's *Women of Algiers*; she reports that Picasso spoke of wanting to paint such a subject himself.[19] In December 1954 Picasso began his reinvention of Delacroix's harem scene in a series of fifteen paintings, whose evolution has been brilliantly analyzed by Leo Steinberg.[20] This immersion produced many drawings and prints, including two lithographs (cats. 35 and 36).

One factor in Picasso's attraction to the subject was his recognition of Delacroix's daring in crossing a cultural barrier by entering the forbidden grounds of a harem. Another was the death in November 1954 of his great colleague Matisse—the only artist Picasso considered his equal.[21] Paying homage to Matisse by way of Delacroix, Picasso said, "When Matisse died, he left his odalisques to me as a legacy."[22] A further factor was the arrival of a new mistress, Jacqueline Roque, whom he married in 1961. She appears as the model for the odalisque seated at the left and in subsequent variations on paintings by Velázquez and Manet, in which the relationship of artist and model was pivotal.[23]

In late 1957 and early 1958, as well as in later years, Picasso often portrayed Roque, his constant companion and admiring audience, who was never far from her chair in his studio.[24] She is shown seated, reading a book in the portrait *Woman with Flowered Blouse* (cat. 41), in which Picasso achieved diverse and subtle tonal effects. It is among his last major lithographs.

LINOCUTS OF THE LATE 1950S AND EARLY 1960S

Spending more time in the South of France in the 1960s, Picasso again used lithography only in minor ways—in some caricatural scribbles, book illustrations, and poster designs. He turned instead to a new medium, the simple—even primitive—linoleum block and, with great ingenuity, subverted the process. These large linocuts, well matched to the intense sunlight of the Mediterranean coast, display a holiday or vacation mood, as do the playful ceramics on which he was also at work. The decorated plates, jars, and plaques were published in editions—another form of printmaking in which a plaster serves as the matrix. The plasters were worked with gravers and gouges similar to those used for linocuts. Picasso's linocuts and ceramics display a bright palette and bravura brushwork. In each case the artist worked closely with one artisan: all

FIGURE 4
**VARIATION ON MANET'S
"DEJEUNER SUR L'HERBE"** (cat. 49)
July 4 and November 23–24, 1961
Linocut printed in black

the linoleum cuts were made in Cannes working with the printer Hidalgo Arnéra, and the ceramics at the Madoura pottery workshop in Vallauris with Georges and Suzanne Ramié.

Among the linocuts, whose subjects include bullfights and decorative heads, is one based on Manet's *Déjeuner sur l'herbe* (fig. 4). As early as 1940 and again from 1959 to 1961, Picasso drew and painted variants of this seminal subject, and in 1962 he made a series of close to a hundred drawings—his last sustained encounter with the work of another great painter.[25]

The complex motives for Picasso's intense dialogues with works by Velázquez, Delacroix, and Manet have been extensively analyzed.[26] Among explanations offered, certain threads are undeniable: parody, a challenge to meet or better his predecessors, new source material, and, perhaps most profoundly, the loneliness of a great artist and the need to communicate with his forebears. Hélène Parmelin wrote, "Picasso often says that when he paints, all the painters are with him in his studio. . . . A solitary painter is never alone."[27] Picasso's final decade of printmaking is replete with elliptical references to past painters.

Bullfighting reemerged as a major theme in Picasso's prints of the late 1950s. In several large linocuts, bull and matador are seen at close range (cats. 43–45), whereas in twenty-six small aquatint plates, published in book form as *La Tauromaquia* (cat. 38), scenes are taken from a more distant vantage point. In choice of subject Picasso pays homage to Goya, but where Goya's scenes are tense, realistic, and often bloody encounters, Picasso's lightly drawn aquatints convey a festive spirit, more like the choreography of a ballet than a dance of death.

SUITE 347 OF 1968

By the mid-1960s Picasso was in his eighties and many of his friends and fellow artists had died: the poet Paul Eluard in 1952; Matisse, Derain, Henri Laurens, Maurice Raynal in 1954; Braque and Cocteau in 1964; and André Breton in 1966. Early in 1968 Jaime Sabartés died. Picasso's friend from Barcelona days, he had long served as secretary and companion. After Sabartés's death, Picasso returned to printmaking, choosing intaglio, a technique in which he worked with greatest ease and rapidity, to review his life and work. His new collaborators were the printers Aldo and Piero Crommelynck at Mougins. *Suite 347* was exhibited and published in 1968–69; a second series of 156 prints was published after the artist's death in 1973.

The first print in *Suite 347* establishes the subject—Picasso observing his life and work (fig. 5). Always conscious of his short stature, here he appears childlike in size, standing next to a magician and watching a performance in a circus setting (cat. 53.1).[28] Other scenes follow the form of a theatrical review in which a chorus alternates with a single voice, and the tone veers from parody to irony. The cast includes expected acrobats and clowns but also introduces drivers of Roman chariots (cat. 53.5). The old Spanish tale *The Celestina* (cats. 53.13 and 53.15) is recast; there is a fleeting reference to Balzac (cat. 53.10). Other scenes are set in the artist's studio, a stage where past and present, family and friends, mingle with fantasies.[29] Memories of his father form one leitmotif, references to the old masters another. The tone changes abruptly, from elliptical and autobiographical references to a brutal rape, drawn in a vigorous, if sometimes shaky, shorthand. In his stream-of-consciousness musings—erotic, often explicit, voyeurism—whatever the subject, Picasso is never far from center stage, even when seeming to be in the wings.

FIGURE 5
**PICASSO, HIS WORK,
AND HIS PUBLIC** (cat. 53.1)
March 16–22, 1968
Etching
From *Suite 347*

FIGURE 1
NORTON SIMON AT HIS HOME IN MALIBU, 1972
NORTON SIMON ART FOUNDATION

NORTON SIMON: COLLECTING AND THE TASTE FOR PICASSO

GLORIA WILLIAMS
CURATOR
NORTON SIMON MUSEUM

Nobody believes me, but the fact is that I never have a fixed
idea about where I am going. I follow the road with the
unknown end. I go where the going looks best.[1]

This quotation from Norton Simon was made as he reflected on his activities as a businessman and industrialist. It rings equally true for his activity as an art collector and his expansive range as a connoisseur. His requirements for art were quality, rarity, beauty, and authenticity. With these criteria, Norton Simon created one of the most important and admired private art collections in the United States. In thirty years he brought together paintings and sculpture from the 14th through the 20th centuries, created one of the preeminent private collections of Indian and Southeast Asian art in the world, and formed a substantial print collection with major holdings of work by history's greatest painter-engravers—Rembrandt, Goya, and Picasso. It is no exaggeration to state that Simon was among the foremost collectors of fine art in the world from 1960s to the mid-1980s (fig. 1).

Simon did not suddenly appear as an imposing presence in the art world, but he quickly evolved into one. He became interested in art casually, as an amateur, and soon matured into a savvy player in the international art market. What stands out in this development is how consuming an adventure and pursuit it became for him in so short a time. As one commentator noted in 1965, Simon "himself is no longer quite sure whether he is an art connoisseur who engages in business or a businessman who collects art."[2] Even Simon's closest friends were prone to descriptions that blurred the boundaries between his business and art interests. Franklin Murphy, former chancellor of the University of California at Los Angeles, who worked with Simon during the latter's tenure on the board of regents for the University, is quoted as saying, "Most businessmen tend to be rather traditional and representational in their approach to business. But I think of Norton as a Cézanne or Picasso, unconventional, constantly probing, testing and continually dissatisfied."[3]

Simon entered the rarefied world of collecting and connoisseurship serendipitously, but for purely practical reasons. Since the 1930s his attentions had been dedicated to his professional life. He served either as chief executive, president, or board member of numerous companies, including Hunt Foods, Ohio Match Company, McCall's Publishing, and various other entities. It was the construction of a new home in 1954 that inspired him to seek out works of art to complete its furnishing. Walking through a Los Angeles gallery with this idea in mind, he noted a late Renoir portrait of a woman entitled *Andrea in Blue*.[4] It became his first acquisition and marked the beginning of a passionate engagement with art and the art market.

In examining the growth of the Simon collection, few patterns are hard, fast, or definitive. The paintings he acquired are chronologically broad in scope and catholic in taste. High-risk acquisitions, in this writer's opinion, took place in the arena of old-master painting. Simon possessed an eye not only for the stunning but also for the exceptional, which enabled him to acquire unexpected and grand compositions by little-known artists. Georg Pencz's *Woman Sleeping (Vanitas)* or Guido Cagnacci's *Martha Rebuking Mary Magdalene for Her Vanity* (fig. 2), for example, were far from conventional acquisitions when they were purchased in 1973 and 1982.[5] On other occasions, Simon found equally surprising, unusual masterpieces by well-known, even popular artists such as the life-size *Penitent St. Jerome* by Francisco de Goya or *The Ragpicker* by Edouard Manet.[6] The Museum's sculpture collection, on the other hand, is primarily modern in character, with a concentration of late 19th- and early 20th-century sculptors, especially Aristide Maillol, Auguste Rodin, and Henry Moore. If any pattern or emphasis can be charted in Norton Simon's collecting, perhaps it lies in his tendency to concentrate on the work of particular artists. Francisco de Zurburán, for example, was an artist rarely sought out by American collectors during the 20th century, yet Simon acquired four paintings by this Spanish

FIGURE 2
Guido Cagnacci (1601–1663),
**MARTHA REBUKING MARY
MAGDALENE FOR HER VANITY,
1661**
Oil on canvas
229.4 x 265.5 cm
NORTON SIMON ART FOUNDATION

master, each a different type of subject, including one of the artist's rare still lifes, *Lemons, Oranges, and a Rose.*[7] Works by Degas, by contrast, have been avidly sought and treasured throughout our century. Nevertheless, in just fifteen years, Simon succeeded in gathering seventy-three sculptures and thirty-one paintings, drawings, and pastels in what is one of the most extensive and diverse collections of Degas's art in any American institution.

This concentration on the oeuvre of individual artists is most apparent in the graphics collection. Given the eclectic taste he demonstrated through his painting acquisitions, it is curious that Simon focused his sights so definitively in the area of print collecting. Yet, within these parameters, he assembled a singular representation of the graphic works of Rembrandt, Goya, and Picasso, each of whom was known for his persistent and pioneering experiments in this medium and for his devotion to the human form.

Simon's interest in the art of Pablo Picasso was long and sustained. In 1962 he purchased his first Picassos, three watercolors.[8] His last Picasso purchase came in 1984 with the acquisition of a lithograph, the fifth state of *The Bull* (cat. 15.3). And over twenty-some years, hundreds of prints, paintings, and sculptures by Picasso were acquired. Today the Picasso holdings in the Museum include five paintings, eight bronzes, and 710 graphic works, including several suites from illustrated books, as well as rare trial and working proofs and progressive states. On these merits alone, the print collection stands as one of the great repositories of the artist's graphic work in the United States. It is a collector's dream, and it is surely a curator's delight with endless possibilities for study, education, and exhibition.

The definitive plunge for collecting Picasso's graphic work occurred in January 1964, when Simon seized the opportunity to purchase one hundred linocuts from a private Swiss collection through Marlborough Gallery in London. The acquisition was noteworthy precisely because the linocuts were not created by the artist as a single suite but represented a protracted exploration of the medium that resulted in new, fresh, and vibrant works. Picasso produced forty-five linocuts between 1958 and 1960, two in 1961, forty-two in 1962, and another eleven in 1963.[9] The purchase heralded another characteristic of Simon's collecting, particularly as it applied to prints: the taste for buying *en masse*, sets, illustrated books, and suites rather than piecemeal. In 1977, for example, Simon purchased 118 Rembrandt etchings assembled by Charles Cunningham, then considered one of the finest print collections by this artist in private hands.[10] Etchings by Goya were acquired with equal zeal. Between 1960 and 1980, Simon purchased six editions of *Los Caprichos* (1799), nine editions of *La Tauromaquia* (1816), five editions of *Los Disastros* (1863), and five first editions of *Los Proverbios* (1864). An apocryphal tale exists that Simon even tried to corner the market on Goya etched suites. Certainly the momentum and ambition of his purchases raise curiosity about that possibility. There was, of course, much appeal to buying in quantity. In comparison with paintings, prints were affordable, and acquiring an entire set provided the sense of money well-spent. Such purchases provided the raw material of press releases, stimulated public curiosity, and formed the basis of exhibitions.

Illustrated books as vehicles of artistic expression were similarly attractive to Simon. He acquired five examples from among the numerous books that Picasso illustrated, including Honoré de Balzac's *Le Chef-d'oeuvre inconnu* (cat. 5), *Les Métamorphoses* by Ovid (cat. 6), and *La Tauromaquia* (cat. 38). The latter, published in 1959 by José Delgado, alias Pepe Illo, was acquired in 1973. This artist's book, part of a deluxe set, had belonged to Georges Bloch, Picasso's friend and author of a catalogue of his graphic production.[11] As a topic for artists, the bullfight had a long history. Picasso returned to the theme repeatedly and embraced the imagery of the bullfight as both naturalistic phenomena (fig. 3) and allegory (cat. 9). Simon seems to have taken equally great interest in it, judging from the wealth of prints on the subject he assembled. By the time Picasso's *Tauromaquia* had entered the collection, Simon had already acquired two copies of the first edition and one of the third of *La Tauromaquia* by Goya. Several years later Simon purchased a suite of prints illustrating the moves, or s*uertes*, of the bullfight by Antonio Carnicero, a contemporary of Goya who made highly popular illustrations of the sport.[12] The fruitful comparisons that resulted from such acquisitions were surely not lost on Simon, and he, in fact, encouraged his curators to create exhibitions that would articulate the prints' similarities and points of departure.

The *Suite Vollard* (cat. 8), Picasso's earliest large and self-referential masterpiece in the graphic medium, entered the collection in 1969. As a set, it represented the culmination of the various themes and artistic experiments that Picasso had undertaken in his earlier print series. The set Simon acquired contained nine proof impressions included among the one hundred etchings, drypoints, and aquatints. Nine years later, Simon had the unparalleled opportunity to best this acquisition. The telling of this adventure gone awry illustrates the often idiosyncratic methods he employed in collecting art. In 1978 Simon entered into negotiations for a precious, complete edition of the *bon à tirer* prints from the *Suite Vollard* from Mme Lacourière, the wife of Roger Lacourière, who had printed the edition of Vollard. (*Bon à tirer*, or ready to print, is the proof selected by the artist among different trials as the best, in his opinion, to serve as the model for the entire printing.) As Mme Lacourière communicated to Simon, this was "the only set of Vollard prints Picasso looked at, approved, held in his hand and signed before the edition was printed."[13] This set was without peer and eminently desirable by the standards that Simon required: unquestionable authenticity and supreme quality. Simon was indeed interested and placed the funds for their purchase in an escrow account. However, as was his custom, Simon prolonged negotiations for the prints over two months. When he requested that eight of the one hundred prints be sent to California for further consideration (from the seller's point of view, a misfortune to one of the eight would damage the integrity of the entire suite), it effectively canceled further discussions of the purchase. Mme Lacourière refused to separate the suite despite the "business formalities that are normal in dealing with a man of his background," as one intermediary put it to her. She responded to Simon with an ultimatum—buy or lose. A total of four months of negotiations had produced nothing, and Simon himself evidently could not see the ramifications of the terms he had established for the prize.

Simon loved the art of negotiating, of making a deal. Occasionally, as explained above, this love worked against him. In most cases, however, it worked to his benefit. One can see from his letters and communiqués to and from dealers the often complex terms he established as part of the negotiations. He might ask to keep an object under consideration and on reserve for long periods of time. This presented quite an obstacle to dealers who, during this reserve period, could not market the object elsewhere. Or, Simon might ask to pay only a portion of the price with the remaining value of the object taken in trade from something in his collection. Nonetheless, Simon enjoyed a reputation in the art market as an astute and discriminating collector who was willing to pay for an object when it met his criteria. It was also known that Simon was willing to

FIGURE 3
Pablo Picasso
THE LANCE
October 13, 1959
Color linocut in gray and black
53.2 x 64.0 cm
Baer 1243 III.B.a; Bloch 920
NORTON SIMON ART FOUNDATION

FIGURE 4
Pablo Picasso
HEAD OF A WOMAN
November 10, 1948
Lithograph in wash drawing on zinc
44.7 x 63.5 cm
Mourlot 122
NORTON SIMON ART FOUNDATION

sell when he deemed the financial rewards to be worthwhile. He regularly requested updates on current market values for the Picasso prints and paintings. In 1980 he entertained the notion of selling the *Suite Vollard* to a private party. In 1982 he sold *Nude Combing Her Hair* (1906), an important early precursor to *Les Desmoiselles d'Avignon*.[14] Although Simon prized and admired the works that he collected, he did not hold romantic notions about them and recognized their market value as a substantive part of their history and importance. More than once Simon expressed surprise that students of art appeared unaware of the monetary value of objects. On one occasion, while walking through a newly installed gallery of 19th-century paintings, he noticed that the Georges Seurat *Stonebreakers Le Raincy* (1882) had been placed near the end of the wall. He promptly requested it be placed in the center of the gallery because it was one of the most expensive paintings in that room.

Simultaneous with the purchase of suites and illustrated books, Simon continued to acquire numerous individual prints and groups of etchings, including 110 selections from the *Suite 347* (cat. 53) and several of Picasso's more adventurous and experimental etchings, such as *The Diver*, printed over collaged papers (cat. 7), and two unique proofs of *Head of a Woman, No. 3 (Dora Maar)* (cat. 13). The sheer number of prints arriving in Los Angeles, notwithstanding their importance and quality, was a cause for wonder. One hastens to add that the prints consumed only a portion of Simon's attention as he continued to purchase major European paintings and sculpture and, by 1972, had expanded his interests to encompass Southeast Asian art.[15]

The highest volume of Picasso prints to enter the collection at one time occurred in 1977, when Simon acquired some 300 prints. Among these were 228 lithographs purchased directly from Fernand Mourlot through Heinz Berggruen's Paris gallery. Mourlot was the master printer who had initially suggested to Picasso that he investigate the lithographic process as a means to reproduce some of his paintings. The medium came to fascinate Picasso, and he soon began to experiment with lithography for its own sake. He worked intensely with Mourlot and

FIGURE 5
Pablo Picasso
**"WOMEN OF ALGIERS"
(AFTER DELACROIX). I**
1955
Oil on canvas
97 x 129.5 cm
NORTON SIMON ART FOUNDATION

his workshop during the late 1940s.[16] Of this group of prints, 168 are signed *bon à tirer*, and another seven carry a signed dedication to the printer (cats. 24 and 27). Particularly important are the numerous subjects shown in progressive states (cats. 14.1–14.4 and 23.1–23.3) and a selection of trial proofs that were not editioned (cat. 15.2).

Picasso's signed *bon à tirer* (*BAT*) impressions, as mentioned earlier, are both important documents—an authorization to Mourlot to print the specified editions—and unique works of art: a *BAT* impression is the only print preceding the edition to have this designated signature by the artist. Some of the lithographs stand apart because, contrary to Picasso's *BAT* indications, an edition was never run off. In some instances, this was due to the deterioration of the stones or zinc plates, as with *Head of a Woman* (fig. 4). Besides this *BAT* lithograph, only five proofs remain. In other cases, the artist presumably changed his mind, as with *Bust in Profile*, third state (cat. 40), from which no edition was ever pulled. This *BAT* proof is the only record of its having been created.

Simon favored certain lithographs because they related to other areas of his collecting interest. Picasso's improvisations entitled *Women of Algiers* after Eugène Delacroix's (1834, Musée du Louvre) are among these. Only five artist's proofs were pulled of each of the five lithographs (cat. 36). Since no editions exist, they are indeed rare. Coincidentally, Simon possessed, since 1973, one of Picasso's painted meditations on the theme, *"Women of Algiers". I* (fig. 5). These paintings too had their genesis in Picasso's reaction to Delacroix.[17] Just as Picasso had been preoccupied with the theme as treated by his predecessor Delacroix, so Simon appears to have been captivated by the images reflecting Picasso's own obsession.

The relationship between an artist and his forebears fascinated Simon. On several occasions he exercised his collecting power to bring together examples of artists conversing with each other across time. For example, Simon's favorite Picasso linocut was *Portrait of a Young Woman* after Lucas Cranach the Elder (cat. 42). Among his paintings, he prized the large and highly unusual Degas *Rape of the Sabines* after Poussin, Rubens's *Sebastian Munster* after Joos van Cleve, Seurat's *Angelica Chained to the Rock* after Ingres, and Redon's *Vase of Flowers* copied after Cézanne's *Vase of Flowers*, the latter of which he also owned.[18]

Simon was likewise attracted to the visual image worked through successive states. His patient and tenacious pursuit of "the complete record" of serial images is demonstrated repeatedly in the collection. Six examples of Picasso's lithograph *Still Life with Fruit Stand* (fig. 6) are illustrative of Simon's method. Created over a ten-day period in November 1945, the series conveys the vigor and animation of Picasso's experiments between Cubist abstraction and traditional representation.[19] The first state is known only through trial proofs, one of which Simon bought in 1969. He acquired the second trial proof of this state in 1977 from P. & D. Colnaghi, London. In the same year, as part of the Mourlot acquisition, he secured the final and remaining trial proof of the first state, along with reserved proofs from the second and third states. Finally, another prime example of the third state, from the edition of fifty, was obtained at

FIGURE 6
Pablo Picasso
STILL LIFE WITH FRUIT STAND
November 6, 1945
Lithograph on stone with crayon,
ink, and scrapings
34.5 x 24.5 cm
Mourlot 6, first state, trial proof
NORTON SIMON FOUNDATION

auction in 1978. As a group, any combination of the first three states is extremely rare. To have literally cornered the market on all three first-state proofs is nothing short of miraculous. It indicates that over nine years, in addition to hundreds of art purchases, and whatever business was at hand, Simon kept his eyes open for the details. This is not an isolated example. Similar pursuits are documentable in other areas of his print collecting, notably in regard to Rembrandt and Goya.

Simon never articulated a philosophy that guided his acquisition of Picasso prints. On the one hand, the number of unique and *bon à tirer* impressions in his collection indicates that he preferred singular works that were above comparison. On the other hand, his purchase of the artist's graphic work *en masse* suggests a fundamentally acquisitive approach. No doubt the motive for his actions lies somewhere in between. As this essay's opening quotation intimates, the acquisitions were to some degree a matter subject to the opportunity of the moment. Yet this wealth of graphic works by one artist, and in this case a man considered one of the titans of modern art, also testifies to Simon's prowess and determination as a collector. His concentration on Picasso as printmaker was not as encyclopedic as it could have been and was, in fact, with Rembrandt, whose entire graphic oeuvre totals fewer than three hundred etchings. Instead, Picasso's appeal for Simon may be explained by a kindred tendency to self-reflection. There is a great deal of personal history in Picasso's graphic works, from the *Suite Vollard* to the *Suite 347*. The suggestion of intimacy, at one moment candid, at another metaphorical, intrigued Simon and surely exercised a great pull on the collector who viewed art as a form of personal communication between artist and viewer. Norton Simon's sentiments about art are perhaps best summed up in his own words, "You see creativity, you see this man spent his whole life painting. You wonder what that expression meant to him and you wonder what your expression means to you . . . what is my life expressing?"[20]

FIGURE 1
INTERIOR SCENE 1926
Lithograph
22.5 x 27.9 cm
Mourlot XXI

PICASSO'S LITHOGRAPHS, 1945–1949

CLINTON ADAMS

On November 2, 1945, Picasso began a period of intensive work at the Imprimerie Fernand Mourlot on the rue de Chabrol, near the Gare de l'Est in Paris, and in the ensuing four months created a series of lithographs that are without precedent either in his work or in the history of lithography. Never had the diverse range of the transfer process been more vividly demonstrated; never had such remarkable works been made on zinc plates; and never had an artist so richly explored the medium's unique capacity to permit a progressive evolution of an image, while preserving and recording it at every step along the way.

All of this was quite unexpected. Previously—more than fifteen years earlier—Picasso had made only twenty-seven lithographs. Examining those works, one senses that, partly because he had not established a true collaboration with a printer, he felt no real engagement with the process.[1] The earliest of those lithographs, intended for publication in books or exhibition catalogues, were drawn with pen or crayon on lithographic transfer paper; then, beginning in 1921, Picasso drew directly on stone. He made a number of solidly composed prints, including *Interior Scene* of 1926 (fig. 1), but none were technically adventurous.

During 1930 (the year in which he made the last of his early lithographs), Picasso was occupied with the etchings for Ovid's *Métamorphoses*; simultaneously, he was making the first of the hundred etchings that would ultimately be grouped together as the *Suite Vollard*. Beginning in 1932 or 1933, Picasso worked with the accomplished intaglio printer Roger Lacourière,[2] a collaboration that greatly extended the range and depth of his printmaking skills and laid the foundation for his later work with Mourlot. In the masterful prints of the *Blind Minotaur* (cats. 8.15–8.17), Picasso worked subtractively with a scraper, exploring the complex possibilities of "negative" drawing—a technique that encompasses both the bleak, abraded surface of *Blind Minotaur Guided by a Little Girl with Pigeon* (cat. 8.16) and the rich, velvety depth of *Blind Minotaur Guided by Marie-Thérèse with a Pigeon* (cat. 8.17): two remarkable prints which, though similar in subject and composition, are miles apart in content and meaning. It was in prints such as these, Pat Gilmour observes, that Picasso developed "an awareness of the expressive possibilities latent in technique itself, an awareness that ensures 'original prints' in the most profound sense of that rather hackneyed phrase, rather than prints that are essentially reproduced drawings."[3] And it was with the experience thus gained that he renewed his exploration of lithography at the Mourlot workshop in November 1945.

During the spring and summer of that year, Picasso's ten-year relationship with Dora Maar had become increasingly precarious, but in August he had gone with her to Cap-d'Antibes, interrupting a developing affair with the young Françoise Gilot. In the fall, alone, and back in Paris, he was distracted from his work by "an increasing flow" of postwar visitors to his studio in the rue des Grands-Augustins. Gilot, who would years later write a book describing her life with Picasso, suggests that such distractions may have provoked him to seek "the relative seclusion of Mourlot's printshop."[4] Other accounts suggest that it was a need to escape the winter cold that sent Picasso to Mourlot, but this cannot be right,[5] for, as Gilot says, the shop "was always rather dark, damp, and cool because if it had been kept comfortably warm, the wax in the lithographic ink would have flowed too freely and direct sunlight would have made the stones and the paper too dry."[6]

Stimulated by Braque's high praise for Mourlot, it is more likely that Picasso simply decided to make lithographs. Thus, when the printer came to his studio one morning, "Picasso listened attentively to the master lithographer's technical explanations, and told him, 'I'll be there day after tomorrow.'"[7]

Because Picasso had never before participated in the daily activities of a lithography workshop, his first days at Mourlot's shop were a time of discovery. From accounts provided by those who observed him at work—Gilot, Mourlot, and his printers—we can reconstruct a vivid picture. The shop itself, as Gilot describes it, "was a dim, cluttered, ramshackle place, full of piles of posters, lithographic stones, and general confusion."[8] There were several pressrooms, known irreverently to regulars as "heaven, purgatory, and hell."[9] Picasso, naturally, was ensconced in heaven, where he "found a quiet corner" and was joined by his printers, Jean Célestin and Père Tutin, "one of the 'grand old men' of the establishment."[10]

> We gave him a stone [Célestin told Hélène Parmelin] and two minutes later he was at work with crayon and brush. There was no stopping him. . . . We used to leave at 8 at night and he would be there at 8:30 in the morning. Sometimes I would suggest that we should call it a day. . . . He would look at a stone, light up a Gauloise and give me one, and then we were off again. . . . Then at night at home he would make a litho on transfer paper on his kitchen stove and in the morning we would start again.[11]

Gilot adds:

> He would greet all the workmen, shake hands with them and call them by their first names. . . . They were a sharp-tongued but friendly crowd, disorderly almost to the point of anarchy. All but one. At the back, in the darkest of the cubicles, worked an old man named Monsieur Tuttin [sic]. For the skillful printing of the most technically exacting work he had no peer. He didn't have the sloppy, anarchic appearance of most of Mourlot's employees. He looked like an elderly accountant out of a Dickens novel, with his sharp blue eyes, steel-rimmed spectacles, pointed features, white hair, and carefully buttoned, neatly pressed black suit. . . . The difficulty was, Monsieur Tuttin did not like Pablo's work. In fact he detested it.[12]

The nature of lithography is such that the skills of sensitive and experienced printers are critical to the process. In relief and intaglio printmaking, the image is physically established in the printing matrix and is thus relatively invulnerable to damage by procedural mistakes at the press;

in lithography, by contrast, the surface of the stone or plate remains essentially flat, and the image and non-image areas are separated chemically from one another. Although the chemistry of lithography is simple in principle—resting on the fact that grease and water will not mix—it is infinitely subtle and complex in application. Transfer lithography differs from direct lithography in that the artist makes his image on a surface, usually a specially prepared sheet of paper, other than that from which it will be printed. When the drawing is placed against the surface of a freshly grained stone or plate and run through the press, the greasy content of the drawing materials is transferred to the receptive surface of the printing element.[13]

When an artist draws directly on a lithograph stone, whether with crayon or wash, the granular (and, in microscopic terms, quite rough) surface of the stone separates the drawing material into tiny particles that cling to the peaks and crevices of the grained surface, creating myriad minute black dots and white interstices which, when etched, become chemically different one from the other.[14] The etch used in lithography—a solution of acidified gum arabic—does not bite into the stone; instead, it serves chemically to separate the image and non-image areas. After etching, the stone is "washed out" and "rolled up," so as to replace the artist's drawing materials with printing ink.[15]

During all these steps, images are easily lost as a consequence of misjudgments: even more so when an artist departs—as Picasso would insist on doing—from the known territory of traditional lithographic methods and procedures. Picasso listened to his printers, but then did as he wished.

Among the unconventional techniques he employed, the one that caused his printers their greatest problem was his incessant reworking of his stones and plates with blades, scrapers, and strong solvents (including gasoline), sometimes totally changing the image. Such major alterations, coming after the stone has been etched, disrupt the physical and chemical integrity of the surface, which will be further endangered by the counteretching needed for addition of

FIGURE 2
HEAD OF A WOMAN
November 2, 1945
Lithograph
34.8 x 25.7 cm
Signed and annotated: *Bon à tirer*
JENNIFER JONES SIMON COLLECTION

new work. Once the original grain has been destroyed, it is more difficult during printing to retain the even film of water that is essential to the process; in extreme cases, some parts of the drawing may have been so gouged and scraped that areas or lines print by relief rather than lithographically. Mourlot tells us that for all these reasons Père Tutin "did not always agree with what was happening and did not hesitate to voice his misgivings."[16] Whatever his "misgivings" (a classic understatement)—actually, his contempt for Picasso's work—Tutin took obstinate pride in printing whatever "impossible" stone was brought his way. Mourlot's colorist, Charles Sorlier, "says he has never encountered anyone as bigoted and stupid as Tutin"; but, he concedes, without him, "an important part of Pablo's work would, perhaps, not exist. One must tip one's hat to him."[17]

Beginning on November 2, 1945, and continuing through February 21, 1946, Picasso worked steadily and intensively at the Mourlot shop, as if mining the lithographic medium in search of its essential character. On the first day he brought with him a small collage made of pieces of inked paper, pasted together to form *Head of a Woman* (fig. 2), and watched with "visible stupefaction" while it was expertly transferred to stone and printed by Père Tutin.[18] Other transfers followed, then some drawings directly on stone. Almost from the first, Picasso developed these prints in multiple states, working closely with Tutin and Célestin to proof an image, then rework it, then rework it again, thus simultaneously preserving and destroying it.

"A picture is a sum of destructions," he had said long before.[19] Then (speaking of his unfinished painting *The Charnel House*): "If it were possible, I would leave it as it is, while I began over and carried it to a more advanced state on another canvas. Then I would do the same thing with that one. There would never be a 'finished' canvas, but just the different 'states' of a single painting, which normally disappear in the course of work."[20]

Both remarks—particularly the latter, made in July 1945, only months before beginning work with Mourlot—serve to illuminate the attitude with which Picasso approached lithography. He moved restlessly back and forth from one stone to another, often working on several lithographs on a single day. He took up subjects, put them aside, began others and put those aside, sometimes for days or weeks. "He worked like a madman," Mourlot has said, "and he who generally got up, like many Spaniards, about 11:30 or 12:00, he was at the workshop at nine o'clock in the morning on the dot. . . . No one knew where Picasso was—he was at the Mourlot workshop for four months, every day but Sunday, he was there."[21]

Uncharacteristically, Picasso dated only a few of the images he made during these sixteen weeks[22]—a total of one hundred states of thirty-seven lithographs (Mourlot 1–37); we thus rely on Mourlot's catalogue (despite some problems and uncertainties)[23] for information about the sequential development of two important lithographs from the winter of 1945–46, *Two Nude Women* (cat. 14) and *The Bull* (cat. 15). In each of these lithographs Picasso used a familiar subject as a vehicle for exploration of the process, clearly fascinated by the ease with which it was possible—to the dismay of his printers—to make radical changes in his images. *Two Nude Women* reprises the theme and composition of his 1931 drypoint, *Two Nudes Resting* (fig. 3): a seated woman in profile at the left, one hand raised to her chin, the other resting on her knee; a sleeping woman behind her; a drapery at upper right.

Picasso worked on the lithograph sporadically for three months, from its first state on November 10—a tentative and unpromising wash drawing (fig. 4)—to its eighteenth (and final)

FIGURE 3
TWO NUDES RESTING
September 19, 1931
Drypoint
From *Suite Vollard*, plate 10
30 x 36 cm
Baer 210 B.c.
NORTON SIMON FOUNDATION

FIGURE 4
TWO NUDE WOMEN
November 10, 1945
Lithograph
25 x 33 cm
Mourlot 16 state i/xviii

state on February 12, 1946.[24] In its third state, he redrew the seated figure—now clearly Gilot—and clarified both the reclining figure and the drapery; even so, the print remained unresolved. In a failed effort to add color to the image, he drew a second stone, proofed in brown, only to abandon it; but then, following a sixth state on November 26, he left the stone untouched for more than a month. Perhaps not by coincidence, November 26 was also the day that—on her twenty-fourth birthday—Gilot returned after a long absence to the rue des Grands-Augustins.

When at last Picasso resumed work on *Two Nude Women* it was with experience accumulated in the intervening weeks, during which he completed seven states of *The Bull* and sixteen other lithographs, much of which work relates, directly and indirectly, to the ultimate conclusion of *Two Nude Women*. While working on *The Bull*, he had successfully undertaken truly radical changes on the stone. In *Page of Sketches* (fig. 5) and *Bulls, Rams, and Birds* (cat. 16) he had explored alternate methods of drawing on stone and transfer paper, and, in the latter, while musing about birds, had had thoughts that would find expression in the marginal remarques added in state eighteen of *Two Nude Women* (fig. 6).[25]

In this and other late states (cats. 14.3 and 14.4) the lithograph's visible pentimenti, scars of the stone's many wounds, and its eroded textures tell the story of its difficult progress;[26] simultaneously, they carry much of its expressive content. Gilot relates that it was only when Picasso added the remarques of insects and birds to the stone's final state that he came to realize that the sleeping woman was Dora Maar.[27] "He said he had always considered Dora such a Kafkaesque personality,"[28] hence the small but lifelike insects. "The birds in the upper and lower margins were for me," Gilot adds.

On December 5, using wash, Picasso drew the first state of *The Bull* (cat. 15.1): "A magnificent bull, beautifully drawn, noble even."[29] Proofs were pulled. "A week later, he returned and asked for a new stone,[30] redrawing his bull with wash and pen (cat. 15.2), and on December 18 he started all over again. In the third state, the bull was redone using a scraper and then a pen,

FIGURE 5
**PAGE OF SKETCHES
(HEADS OF CHILDREN
AND HORSES)**
December 4, 1945
Lithograph
27.2 x 40.0 cm
Mourlot 18
JENNIFER JONES
SIMON COLLECTION

with great emphasis placed on its bulk, so that it became a terrifying beast with horns and frightening eyes."[31] On December 22 he made the transfer lithograph *Bulls, Rams, and Birds*, which, as we have seen, played a role in his thoughts about *Two Nude Women*. (Here, the bulls face left, as did *The Bull*, when seen on the stone.) On that same date, he carried *The Bull* to state four, the first step in its transition from realism to abstraction. When at Christmas his work at Mourlot's was interrupted by the unwelcome holiday, he continued to develop his conception in the transfer lithograph *Side View of Bull* (cat. 18), which would serve to guide his further revisions of *The Bull*. On December 26, he then eliminated the face that appeared in state five (cat. 15.3)—a face that resembles the bull's head in *Guernica*—and replaced it in state six (cat. 15.4) with a witty, linear abstraction.[32]

In the days that followed, Picasso continued to carve away at his bull until there was very little left, thus confounding his printers:

> At the last proof [Célestin said] there remained only a few lines. I had watched
> him at work, reducing, always reducing. I remembered the first bull and I said
> to myself: What I don't understand is that he has ended up where he really
> should have started! But he, Picasso, was seeking his own bull. And to achieve
> his one-line bull he had gone in successive stages through all the other bulls.
> And when you look at that line you cannot imagine how much work was
> involved.[33]

But of course the final stage is not just the line: it is the character of that fragmented line, drawn on the much-scraped stone; and it is the residue, the many tiny ghosts, of the stages that preceded it. Picasso could not have begun *The Bull* as he ended it.

While working on stones at Mourlot's, Picasso also discovered in the transfer process something more than simple convenience. Using transfers, he could do things not possible on stone: creating new textures through use of frottage—rubbings of irregular surfaces on which the transfer paper might be placed; and cutting and juxtaposing elements of drawings and frottages to create collage-like lithographs that echoed his sculptures, in which, Roland Penrose observes, we experience "the disconcerting quality of a joke that contains serious implications."[34]

We see Picasso's dry wit in his serial destruction of *The Bull* and his mordant humor in the insects that infest the margins of the final state of *Two Nude Women*; but it is in the transfer prints that he most often engages in visual puns and is simply playful: witness *Eight Silhouettes* (cat. 19), in which a procession of cutout female nudes—arms and breasts askew—present themselves in review; and the more complex *Bullfight under a Black Sun* (cat. 17), in which he plays a little game with the viewer. Gilot comments at length on the way in which Picasso in this print adapts the principle of the *papier collé* to lithography; on his combination of frottage with directly drawn elements; and, in particular, on his repetition of the figure of the picador, cut from one place and put in another, thus creating two picadors, one positive, one negative.[35]

FIGURE 6
TWO NUDE WOMEN
February 12, 1946
Lithograph
25.0 x 33.0 cm
Mourlot 16 xviii/xviii
MUSEUM OF MODERN ART,
NEW YORK

After at last finishing his work on *Two Nude Women* on February 12, Picasso spent the next ten days carrying to conclusion some listless experiments with color lithography, drawing several more transfer lithographs, and arranging for the printing of some small studies made along the way (among them two Rorschach-like inkblots that likely infuriated Père Tutin).[36]

With that done, Picasso left the printshop. Only once thereafter, in the winter of 1948–49, would he again immerse himself so deeply and with such continuity in lithography, working directly with his printers. It was in these two periods (and some intervening prints) that Picasso "virtually reinvented the process"[37] and, through the power and richness of his images, set the medium firmly on a new course.

In the summer of 1946 Picasso made a series of transfer lithographs, ten of which were drawn on one day, all portraits of Gilot; then in January 1947 he began a second series. First came several prints of a little owl that had now joined the pigeons and turtledoves in his kitchen menagerie; then several classical subjects, freshly drawn with pen and brush, combined in some with crayon frottage. Technically the most daring of these transfer lithographs was the highly unconventional *Pigeon on Gray Background* (cat. 21). After brushing in a dark background, he painted the image of the pigeon with water-based white gouache, which, of course, separated irregularly, repelled by the greasy black tusche.[38] "When Mourlot . . . saw what Pablo had done, he said, 'How do you expect us to print that? It's not possible'. . . . 'You give it to Monsieur Tuttin [*sic*]; he'll know how to handle it,' Pablo told him."[39] As indeed he did.

The discovery that the lithograph could be printed with "remarkable results" (Mourlot's words) led directly to Picasso's many subsequent explorations of varied resists and stop-outs, which he combined with positive drawing to create effects achievable in no other way.[40] Of the thirty-nine transfer lithographs Picasso made between January 20 and April 18, many were clearly experimental and few were printed in editions.

In early March, Picasso began to work on zinc plates, probably as a means to make it easier to work in his studio rather than at the Mourlot shop. Although widely used in lithography, zinc plates traditionally had been thought to be a lesser alternative to stone, convenient because of their light weight but limited in application and risky at the press. Whereas on stone, the image and non-image areas of a drawing tend to be equally secure, on zinc they are imbalanced: images tend to fill and darken because of the "grease-loving" character of the metal, and some techniques—including the extensive scraping and scratching that Picasso had employed so effectively in *Two Nude Women* and *The Bull*—are both more difficult (zinc is a very hard metal) and more precarious than on stone.[41] In compensation, zinc permits the development of images that cannot be duplicated on stone: smoky, solvent washes, and the broken, granulated water washes—unique to zinc—that lithographers call *peau de crapaud* (literally, "skin of a toad").[42]

As ever, conventional wisdom was of little concern to Picasso. Immediately, he put zinc to the test, simultaneously developing in pen and wash a portrait of Gilot (carried into four

Figure 7
Lucas Cranach the Elder (1472–1553)
DAVID AND BATHSHEBA
1526
Oil on panel
36 x 24 cm
DAHLEM GEMÄLDEGALERIE, BERLIN

states); another portrait and a still life; then the handsome *Composition with Vase of Flowers*, his most successful color lithograph to this date (cat. 22).[43] At month's end he embarked on what would, surprisingly, turn out to be a two-year project: a series of variations on the 16th-century painting *David and Bathsheba* by Lucas Cranach the Elder (fig. 7).[44]

Working again in the Mourlot press-room, Picasso repeatedly revised his initial pen and brush drawing, carrying it through five states, each of which was proofed in sequence. In the process, he greatly altered Cranach's composition (reversed left-to-right in printing): he brought Bathsheba front and center; grouped her attendants more closely; gave David greater prominence, as he peers down from above; and activated Cranach's passive spaces—the sky at upper right, the blank architectural elements, and the dark mass of foliage—integrating them with the figures.

The first, second, and fourth states were pulled in editions (cats. 23.1–23.3); then, after the fifth state, Picasso put the plate aside and left it untouched for a year. Following further alterations, state six was proofed in March 1948 but then—still unresolved—again put aside. Finally, in October, Picasso had the image transferred to a stone.[45] "Taken to the artist's studio," Mourlot writes, "[the stone] was placed on a large cast-iron cooking pot, but Picasso seldom went near it. 'It frightens me, I dare not touch it,' he told me when I inquired about it. However, the stone was attacked once more, worked on and scraped; one day some retouching with a pen, and the next day a long session of scraping, then a reworking of the blacks, etc. Picasso would no doubt still be working on it if, having to leave for the South of France at the beginning of June 1949, he had not asked that the stone be removed and a proof pulled."[46] Working on the fresh surface of the stone (always a surface more responsive than zinc to the touch of the needle), Picasso achieved a delicate embroidery of intertwined lines and a dramatic rhythm of flickering light.[47] Again the stone was put aside, but Picasso never returned to it.

Some years later when he was working on a series of fifteen paintings, variations on Delacroix's *Women of Algiers* (fig. 8),[48] his memory of the earlier lithograph may have motivated the two lithographic versions of the Delacroix subject, this time working from the start on stone and on a black ground (cats. 35 and 36).

One of Picasso's most ambitious projects from the winter of 1948–49—the group of prints titled *Woman in an Armchair*—resulted from an abandoned attempt to create a complex five-color lithograph: an undertaking inspired by the sight of Gilot wearing a coat he had brought her from Poland: a coat made of brown leather, "decorated with peasant embroidery in red, blue, and yellow and . . . lined with black sheep's wool."[49] But after seeing the proofs, Picasso was struck by the fact that the five plates were individually more interesting in their range of black and gray tones than when printed together in color. In the following weeks, he developed each of the plates separately, some giving birth (through transfer) to still other plates, ultimately resulting in a total of at least twenty-seven images, not all of which were editioned.[50] This series of black-and-white prints, which Brigitte Baer considers "the acme" of Picasso's work in lithography,[51] is represented in this exhibition by the fifth and final state developed from the violet plate (cat. 26).

While working on the many variations of *Woman in an Armchair*, Picasso made other lithographs, working almost exclusively on zinc plates. On January 9 he produced both *The Dove* (cat. 27) and *The Lobster* (cat. 28), and four days later *The Toad* (cat. 29), all drawn with total assurance, but in quite different ways. In *The Dove*, Picasso uses tusche washes diluted with

FIGURE 8
Eugène Delacroix (1798-1863)
WOMEN OF ALGIERS
1834
Oil on canvas
180 x 229 cm
MUSÉE DU LOUVRE, PARIS

gasoline to seduce from the zinc plate qualities unparalleled in lithography, nuances that, miraculously, Tutin managed to preserve at the press.[52] (Scornful to the end, Tutin tore in two the impression of this masterpiece that Picasso gave him in recognition of his achievement.[53]) In *The Lobster*, Picasso draws more directly, contrasting layered strokes of gray and black tusche with brilliant, untouched whites. (The black globules seen in some strokes result from intermixture of solvent- and water-based tusche washes.) In *The Toad*, he makes use of his full technical vocabulary: gum resists, as seen in the white dots and the white brushstrokes at left; soft, pale washes, again diluted with gasoline; tusche, irregularly daubed on the plate, perhaps with wadded-up paper; and superimposed lines, drawn with brush and crayon.

Although after 1949 Picasso continued to make lithographs, the medium was no longer so central to his work. He was spending more time in the South of France, where, despite Mourlot's efforts to ship plates back and forth, he was distant from his printers. With notable exceptions, his lithographs of the 1950s and 1960s lack the power and force of those made between 1945 and 1949.

FIGURE 1
TWO WOMEN LOOKING AT A SCULPTED HEAD (cat. 8.5)
March 21, 1933
Etching
From *Suite Vollard*, plate 42

MARIE-THERESE: A PERFECT ODALISQUE

PAT GILMOUR

So many prints were made in celebration of her charms, that it is difficult to dismiss the idea that in the decade from 1927 to 1937 Picasso's "highly autobiographical" output was "a never-ending lyrical poem" to Marie-Thérèse Walter—the girl who became his muse, his lover, and the mother of his elder daughter.[1]

All the same, art as autobiography has lately been under attack. Adam Gopnik, who was first to spot the disguised initials of Picasso and Marie-Thérèse in some schematic guitars of 1927, warned that there was "more involved in an image than diary keeping." The game of encoding, he said, was part of Picasso's genius, and "being a formalist in spite of himself" was central to his artistic achievement.[2] More recently, Rosalind Krauss, dissecting a sketchbook the artist completed in 1926, argued that it would be far more constructive to analyze Picasso's changing styles than to keep adding details to his biography. The sketchbook she was discussing included several interlaced black-and-white drawings of a girl's head, in which the conflation of full face and profile emerged as a major structural device.[3] The head possessed "a wide, oval face, a Roman nose bridging straight from the forehead, and short, cropped, blond hair." In other words, Krauss reasoned, Picasso had created a doppelgänger for Marie-Thérèse a year before they ever met.[4]

The sketchbook Krauss was investigating led to a monumental painting[5] which—Picasso had told a cataloguer in 1955—featured a milliner's workshop he was able to see from his fourth-floor Paris apartment in rue La Boétie. In his recent essay for the book *Picasso and Portraiture*, William Rubin noted the painting's curvilinear Cubist style and strangely cinematic quality, "combining sensual interlacing arabesques with austere tones of black, gray and white."[6] Rubin also summarized the little-known work of Dr. Herbert T. Schwarz—a Canadian physician and amateur art historian fascinated by Marie-Thérèse—who has mounted a convincing case that she and Picasso met perhaps two years before the accepted date.[7] In truth, the "milliner's workshop," Dr. Schwarz declared, pictured Marie-Thérèse, her mother, and her sister, sewing in their Maisons Alfort home.[8] Convinced by this evidence, Rubin pointed out that the picture also featured an image of the artist "as a mysterious black silhouette entering through the glass-paneled door at right: the door's oversize knob functions as an unmistakable sexual metaphor, which would reappear in Picasso's pictures of Marie-Thérèse for more than a decade."[9]

Despite his fame, Marie-Thérèse had never heard of Picasso when he picked her up on a crowded Paris boulevard one Saturday evening. Nevertheless, she was thrilled to meet a painter, as her mother's great love had been a painter too. Picasso told her: "Madamoiselle, you have an interesting face. I would like to make your portrait." And he added, presciently: "I sense we will do great things together."[10] For Picasso, who was already in his mid-forties, the encounter was in line with the Surrealist conception of an *amour fou*, a love affair with someone who was essentially still a child. Even on January 8, 1927—the date traditionally given for their meeting—Marie-Thérèse was a minor. Yet although she told Pierre Cabanne she was "a good girl"—implying their love was unconsummated until she came of age[11]—she later admitted that she and Picasso were lovers soon after their meeting, by which time the artist's name had become synonymous with secrecy. Although in 1930 Picasso moved Marie-Thérèse into a flat in the street where he and Olga Picasso lived, such was their discretion that his wife suspected nothing until 1932, when paintings of Marie-Thérèse were shown at the Galerie Georges Petit. Forty years later, historians still erroneously believed that Picasso's move to his sculpture studio at Boisgeloup marked the beginning of their liaison.[12]

Despite the fact that prints in multiple impressions have a greater potential to betray a secret than a single painting, it was in graphic art that Marie-Thérèse first unambiguously found her way into Picasso's work. Her full face and profile, typically conflated, appeared as a lithograph in the luxury edition of a book about Picasso's drawings. Offering scant evidence, the catalogue of Picasso's books suggests that the image—of fine lines scratched out of a black ground—should be dated to 1925, although the accompanying text was printed in June 1926.[13] The cataloguer notes, however, that the face "seems to prefigure that of Marie-Thérèse Walter,

FIGURE 2
FACE OF MARIE-THERESE
October 1928
Lithograph
20.4 x 14.2 cm
Baer 243

whom the artist was to meet in January 1927."[14] In 1928 Picasso drew two very different lithographic portraits of his lover, possibly to offer a choice of plates for yet another monograph about him, this time by André Level. The publisher chose *Face of Marie-Thérèse*[15]—a subtle close-up (fig. 2), its eyebrow arched in classical perfection—in preference to the more prosaic and literal alternative.[16]

Marie-Thérèse was first pictured in Picasso's etchings during the early part of 1927. The teenager's short hair and slender body is clearly represented in *The Nude Model*,[17] while the same athletic form—markedly different from earlier turbanned models—also appears in four plates of Honoré de Balzac's *Chef-d'oeuvre inconnu*.[18] The story features a painter called Frenhofer—with whom Picasso was increasingly to identify—who spent a decade trying to achieve the perfect portrait, only to produce an incoherent web of lines.[19] Except for a single illustration, in which the image of a woman knitting is translated into a tangled skein of wool,[20] Picasso refers only obliquely to the story, although other plates hint at the complex interrelationships between artists, models, and paintings. In one, for example, the teenage Marie-Thérèse sits behind the artist while he paints on his canvas the woman she will become. When the book was published in 1931 Picasso framed the table picturing all twelve etchings together, by placing the rangy body of his lover on all four sides.

FIGURE 3
**MAN UNVEILING
A WOMAN** (cat. 8.2)
June 20, 1931
Drypoint
From *Suite Vollard*, plate 5

A lithograph in which Marie-Thérèse poses in front of the easel on a studio chaise longue and departs from behind it as Europa on a bull coincides with the illustrations for Ovid's *Métamorphoses*. According to Brassaï, who photographed the extraordinary sculptures Picasso made of Marie-Thérèse at Boisgeloup, the artist was charmed by her youth, her gaiety, and her laughter and loved "the blond sheen of her hair, her luminous complexion, and her sculptural lines."[21] She was the perfect choice as a model for Ovid's stories, as her classical profile was ideally suited to the writings of a Roman poet. Close-ups of Marie-Thérèse adorn many of the book's half-titles, and the rape of Philomela was clearly informed by her sexual abandon. Huffington, one of Picasso's biographers, who took a jaundiced view of his morality, felt that Ovid's story of Jupiter and Semele could well have been based on the artist and his lover, for when Jupiter appeared in all his splendor, Semele, consumed by his radiance, ended as a pile of ash.[22]

The earliest prints for the *Suite Vollard* alternated during the autumn of 1930 with the plates for Ovid.[23] A run of rather bland sitting or standing nudes was broken in April 1931 by the urgent drypoint of a young man unveiling a sleepy Marie-Thérèse (fig. 3). A year or so later, in his study of a rape, Picasso tore into the metal with the same tool, depicting Marie-Thérèse, eyes shut and head thrown back, in characteristic abandon (cat. 8.7).[24]

A run of prints late in 1932 conveys alarm, panic, and distress. The sense of danger is so palpable that when Mary Matthews Gedo considered the imagery in the book with a psychoanalytic slant that she wrote about Picasso, she theorized that Marie-Thérèse either had attempted suicide or had undergone an abortion. "Certainly," Gedo wrote, "some disaster occurred which impressed Picasso with her vulnerability and his own responsibility to watch over, reassure, and rescue her."[25]

Spurred by Gedo's theory, Brigitte Baer researched the matter for the relevant volume of her catalogue.[26] She knew Marie-Thérèse was an experienced swimmer and proficient in all branches of lifesaving. After jogging the memories of Marie-Thérèse's relatives, Baer discovered

FIGURE 4
THE DIVER (cat. 7)
November 29, 1932
Etching printed over collage of
sand- and salmon-colored papers

that late in 1932, when swimming in the river Marne, she had been infected by a malignant virus normally transmitted by rats. For a time it was feared she would die. During her illness and long convalescence she looked like a skeleton and lost most of her hair. In his works on the theme of *The Rescue of the Drowned Woman* Picasso dealt pictorially with the crisis.[27] Proofed by the artist himself, often crooked on the sheet, smudged, or inadequately inked, the tiny etchings of the period strongly convey his anguish, as does his inventive technique. Instead of employing the traditional feather to sweep away the gases that form on an acid-bitten line, Picasso let the bubbles remain to reinforce the suggestion of drowning. In *The Diver* (fig. 4) Marie-Thérèse plays every role—she swims by, looks on aghast, and executes the diver's vertiginous plunge.[28] With the help of Père Molinier at Roger Lacourière's workshop, Picasso tried out both positive and negative impressions. Others were imposed over shafts of collaged glacé paper or cutouts of his lover's silhouette (cat. 7). Most touchingly of all, he adhered some strips of bandage to one of his trial proofs, and tenderly tinted it with watercolors.[29]

In endless subsequent monotypes, painted in ink on metal and then transferred to paper, Picasso willed his lover to get well, focusing on her vulnerability in a heart shape formed from the profile of her face, even recording the sparseness of her hair. Through January into February 1933 flutists serenade the invalid. She sleeps. Even in March, when bathers play ball,

FIGURE 5
**SCULPTURE. PROFILE
OF MARIE-THERESE**
March 12, 1933
Etching
17.6 x 15.5 cm
Baer 295

Marie-Thérèse sinks exhausted to the foot of the sheet.[30] The healing seems to be nearing completion when Picasso makes several experimental prints based on the sculptures he had made of her (fig. 5). In one dramatic sequence, her mutating head turns through 180 degrees in the course of twenty states.[31] Finally, the artist etched an image of her head on top of a tiny column garlanded with ivy and made a monument of her. Lovingly etching the print through thirteen complex changes, he used his lover's nail polish to resist the acid.[32]

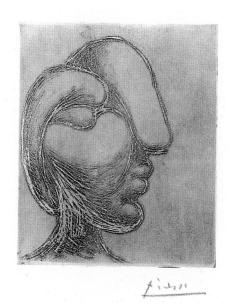

Two years earlier, in May 1931, Picasso had moved into the château de Boisgeloup. Forty miles northwest of Paris, but off the beaten track, it was beyond the range of Olga's wrath. The sculptures of Marie-Thérèse that he made there between 1931 and 1933 have been described as "massive and grave and, for all their originality . . . classical in feel." And despite their blatant sexuality, they radiate "a stately *gravitas*" and "calm, Olympian fulfilment."[33] In mid-March 1933 Picasso resumed the etchings which were to become part of the *Suite Vollard* to make an elegant sequence, drawn in a Neoclassic line, following the fortunes of a bearded sculptor (cats. 8.3–8.6). In two of the sheets the artist looks at a sculpted head of Marie-Thérèse. In another, two girls gaze thoughtfully at the most sexually explicit of the sculptures, with its pronounced nose, softly opened mouth, and an almond eye incised into its cheek (fig. 1). A fourth plate conjures up a three-dimensional version of one of Picasso's drawings, while in a fifth, Marie-Thérèse considers a surreal metamorphosis of herself, made from an assemblage of household objects (cat. 8.8). Throughout the series a vase of

FIGURE 6
**AT THE BATH. WOMAN IN FLOWERED HAT
AND WOMAN WRAPPED IN A TOWEL** (cat. 8.12)
January 29, 1934
Etching
From *Suite Vollard*, plate 79

anemones recurs as a symbol for Picasso's lover. When, his marriage in tatters, the Minotaur decides to leave home at the end of 1934, the vase of flowers is among the pitiful household chattels he takes with him.[34]

When Picasso was courting Françoise Gilot in the 1940s, one of his none too original invitations to her was to come up and see his etchings. In the book she later wrote about their life together, Gilot recorded his running commentary on several of the Vollard plates. Pointing to the image of a draped woman near a companion in a flowered hat (fig. 6), the artist told Gilot: "That's you. You see it, don't you? . . . I've always been haunted by a certain few faces and yours is one of them."[35]

Picasso also told her about the Minotaur, the artist's alter ego. First seen in a painting of 1928, the beast with a man's body and a bull's head began appearing frequently in Picasso's work in 1933, after he had designed a cover for the journal the Surrealists named after the creature. They admired the Minotaur's irrational impulses, but for Picasso he signified passion, artistic vision, and a link between bullfighting and the Greco-Roman tradition. The artist told Gilot that the action in his etchings took place on an island "like Crete." This made it clear that he equated his own story with the myth in which maidens were sacrificed to the Minotaur's appetites, until Theseus, helped by Ariadne, slew him. "After the heat of the day has passed," Picasso explained to Gilot, "they bring in the sculptors and their models for parties, with music and dancing, and everybody gorges himself on mussels and champagne until melancholy fades away and euphoria takes over. From there on it's an orgy."

One print shows Marie-Thérèse watching over the Minotaur, who snoozes behind a diaphanous floral curtain. In another—the tables turned—the beast caresses the hand of the sleeping Marie-Thérèse with his muzzle (fig. 7). "He's trying to decide if she loves him *because* he's a monster," Picasso told Gilot. "Women are odd enough for that you know." Then, looking at the etching again, he added, "It's hard to say whether he wants to wake her or kill her."

In the autumn of 1934, on Picasso's return from a trip to Spain, the theme of the Minotaur was supplanted by the bullfight—one of the artist's lifelong passions. In the opening phase of a corrida, the bull is encouraged to gore the horse's side, which allows the picador, who sits astride the horse, to plant his lance in the bull's neck. This strategy tires the bull and makes it drop its head sufficiently for a matador on foot to kill it. Aficionados usually focus on the ritual fight to the death, but Picasso was always more interested in the interplay between the bull and the horse. The bull, the male principle, attacks the horse, the female principle, in an encounter seen by the artist as a metaphor for sex. This symbolism was even more vivid in the days before horses wore protective padding when, ripped open by the bull's horns, they would spill their entrails on the ground.[36] Moreover, the picador's intervention made each protagonist both torturer and sacrificial victim—a terrible blending of love and destruction that formed the subject matter of two large plates in June and September. In one, Marie-Thérèse and the bull appear to be kissing each other (fig. 8). In the second, bull, torera, and picador are mingled in violent and hideous confusion (cat. 10).[37] This savage theater had its light to shed on Picasso's troubles with his disaffected wife.

Picasso also exorcised his fear that Olga's spleen would damage Marie-Thérèse by appropriating Marat, the revolutionary murdered in his bath, as seen in the 19th-century painting by the French artist Jacques-Louis David. In Picasso's astringent drypoint, Olga as murderess—all savage mouth and teeth—attacks her husband's mistress with a butcher knife. Made for *De derrière les fagots* by the Surrealist poet Benjamin Péret, Picasso drew the tiny image on a plate too large for it. So after it had been editioned for the book, the artist turned the plate upside down, cancelled the earlier image, and etched another in the empty space beside it (cat. 8.15). Just as Ariadne helped Theseus find his way by supplying him with thread, so Marie-Thérèse—as a *femme-enfant* carrying doves or flowers—leads the blind and penitent Minotaur out of the labyrinth (fig. 9).

At the end of 1934, Marie-Thérèse told Picasso she was pregnant. The following spring,

FIGURE 7
**MINOTAUR CARESSING THE HAND OF A
SLEEPING WOMAN WITH HIS MUZZLE** (cat. 8.11)
June 18, 1933 or later
Drypoint
From *Suite Vollard*, plate 93

Picasso brought the story of the Minotaur to its end with *The Minotauromachy*, an etching that ranks as one of the most important prints of this, or of any other, century. In it, Marie-Thérèse, who is clearly several months into her pregnancy, lies across the dying horse. The print brings together both strands of the *Suite Vollard*—the classical sculptor and the Minotaur. A book elaborating twenty-six different interpretations has been devoted to the imagery of *The Minotauromachy*.[38] Alfred Barr, the first art historian to discuss the masterpiece, pointed out the symbols that recurred in it from the artist's earlier work.[39] Nevertheless, he felt it was such an intuitive and personal allegory that even the artist would not—or could not—put it into words. Picasso said as much about *Guernica*, which shares part of the etching's iconography: "This bull is a bull and this horse is a horse. . . . Sure, they're symbols. But isn't it up to the painter to create symbols? Otherwise it would be better if he wrote them out in so many words."[40] By 1936 the Minotaur had disappeared from Picasso's work. In his last and most beautiful fiction for the *Suite Vollard* a rather more civilized handsome young faun looks down on Marie-Thérèse, somnolent in the moonlight (fig. 10).

In 1937, in response to atrocities of the Spanish Civil War, Picasso etched fourteen frames of the two-sheet comic strip *Dreams and Lies of Franco* (cat. 12)[41] to raise funds for the Republican cause. Originally intended to be cut up into eighteen postcards, it shows Franco as an ugly polyp, attacking various Spanish institutions and hacking at a classical bust of Marie-Thérèse with a pick-axe. Four final frames were added to the images on the second sheet after the painting *Guernica* had been completed. In this great work, which expressed horror and indignation at the German bombing of civilians in the Basque town, Marie-Thérèse holds out her lamp in the darkness, while Dora Maar—by now her successor—is weeping.

When Olga left Picasso in 1935, he spent every day with Marie-Thérèse, doing the washing, making the meals, helping her with her daughter. But this domestic interlude soon palled. For shortly after Maya's birth, Picasso met Dora. And Dora, says Richardson, was the reverse of

FIGURE 8
WOMAN BULLFIGHTER, LAST KISS? (cat. 9)
June 12, 1934
Etching

Marie-Thérèse, "dark instead of fair, chic instead of sloppy, tormented instead of placid, intellectual instead of sportive."[42] Later, when Gilot succeeded Maar, Picasso told her that he had not been greatly attracted to Dora. "I just felt that finally, here was somebody I could carry on a conversation with."[43]

After his marriage to Jacqueline Roque, who moved in when Gilot moved out, Picasso's contact with Marie-Thérèse virtually ceased. Throughout the 1940s he kept in touch with his daughter and sent regular checks to Marie-Thérèse. He also gave her proofs of his lithographs as he made them. But a decade later Marie-Thérèse, who had no other man in her life, was frequently in need of money. Frank Perls, a California dealer, witnessed an ugly scene when Jacqueline forbade Picasso to sign some lithographs belonging to Marie-Thérèse, which she had asked Perls to sell to raise money.[44]

Despite the sorrow she must have felt after being discarded, Marie-Thérèse did not suffer quite such a savage process of "psychosexual dissection"[45] as Olga and Dora, although her rare appearances in Picasso's prints after the Second World War are probably not those by which she would choose to be remembered. She takes her place in the major etching that Picasso based on Rembrandt's *Ecce Homo*, in which he reviews the roles he had played in his life, as well as picturing his most important partners. Baer suggests that the girl in a bathtub on the dais refers to Marie-Thérèse as swimmer. She also occurs a second time, turning away from the audience in the lower half of the composition.[46] Her final appearance in the graphic work is as a slapstick torera. The print emerged from the torrent of ribald etchings that poured out of Picasso toward the end of his life. Surrounded by a motley crew of picaresque Spanish characters, Marie-Thérèse swoons inelegantly across the back of a randy horse.[47]

On April 1, 1973, Picasso wrote to Marie-Thérèse, telling her she was the only woman he had ever loved.[48] A week later, he died. By order of Jacqueline, who was known to the family as Cerberus—the monstrous dog that guards the entrance to the Underworld—neither his illegitimate children, his grandchildren, nor, of course, his ex-lovers were allowed into the

FIGURE 9
**BLIND MINOTAUR GUIDED BY A LITTLE
GIRL WITH BUNCH OF FLOWERS** (cat. 8.15)
September 22, 1934
Drypoint, scraper, and burin
From *Suite Vollard*, plate 94

château de Vauvenargues to attend his funeral. So Marie-Thérèse had to beg Picasso's secretary to kiss him for her. Nevertheless, the sculpture the artist chose to stand over his grave was *The Woman with a Vase*—a monumental bronze fertility goddess, based on drawings of Marie-Thérèse made during the halcyon days of their love affair.[49]

In October 1977 when the wrangling about Picasso's estate was over and the illegitimate children were assured of proper recognition, Marie-Thérèse hanged herself in her garage. In a farewell letter to her daughter, Maya, she wrote that she had been overcome by an irresistible compulsion. "It wasn't just his dying that drove her to it," said Maya. "It was much, much more than that. . . . She felt she had to look after him. She couldn't bear the thought of him being alone."[50]

It was in 1935 that Picasso made a statement that gives us a clue as to how the formal qualities in his art related to the people in his life. "Do you think it concerns me," he said, "that a particular picture of mine represents two people? Though these two people once existed for me, they exist no longer. The 'vision' of them gave me a preliminary emotion; then little by little their actual presences became blurred; they developed into a fiction and then disappeared altogether, or rather they were transformed into all kinds of problems. They are no longer two people, you see, but forms and colors: forms and colors that have taken on meanwhile, the idea of two people, and preserve the vibrations of their life."[51]

What is so striking about Picasso's work is the ingenuity with which he devises such appropriate methods to convey his subjective visions. That being so, it follows that the more one knows, not only of the artist but of the people who inspired him, the better the chance of aesthetic understanding. Writing in 1990 about the lyricism radiated by Marie-Thérèse, Gilot said that her sculptural proportions, classical profile, passivity, and voluptuous rhythms had combined to make her "a perfect odalisque. . . . Love and peace are what they are," concluded Gilot, "and as such they endure."[52]

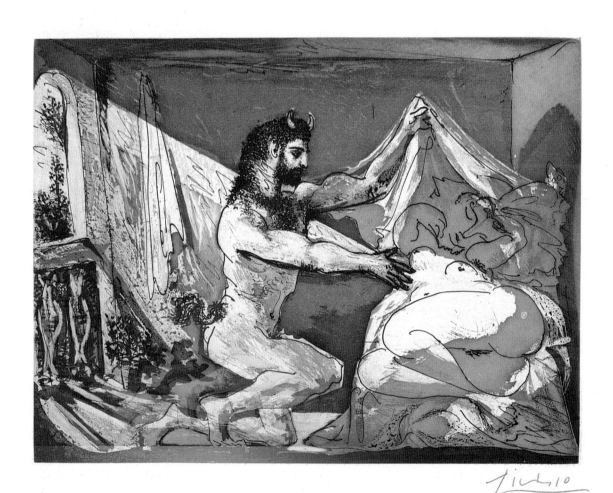

FIGURE 10
FAUN UNVEILING A SLEEPING WOMAN
("JUPITER AND ANTIOPE" AFTER REMBRANDT) (cat. 8.20)
June 12, 1936
Sugar-lift aquatint and scraper
From *Suite Vollard*, plate 27

FIGURE 1
**DOUBLE SELF-PORTRAIT TRANSPOSED AND
DREAMING OF THE CIRCUS WITH JACQUELINE
AS AN ACROBAT, STANDING ON A BALL** (cat. 53.3)
March 26, 1968
Etching
From *Suite 347*

PAINTING AS PERFORMANCE ART: THE CASE OF PICASSO

DAVID CARRIER

Biography is . . . a convenient fiction since no one can probe, without the risk of farcical failure, those hidden perceptions or experiences which run alongside the observable life but may not necessarily touch it.[1]

Consider a small part of the entry in the index to the first volume of John Richardson's *Life of Picasso:*[2]

Picasso, Pablo

as director of Prado,

drawing in sand,

and drugs,

and drunkenness,

earliest sexual experience,

examinations; drawings for,

exemption from military service,

and his father,

first communion,

handwriting analyzed,

height.

Suppose someone knowing nothing of the art of Pablo Picasso were to read the literature on him and to compare it to commentary on other famous artists. We have much personal information about Michelangelo, thanks to his friend Vasari; because Poussin had to deal with geographically distant Parisian patrons, we have his extensive business correspondence. But there exist only incidental written records of Caravaggio and Rembrandt. By the 19th century, detailed records are kept; however private a great artist might be, inevitably information about him is sought out. Cézanne, Degas, and Manet have become, through their interpreters, as familiar to us as the writers of their era. And when we get to the 20th century, elaborate biographies are written about anyone who achieves fame, with even the most trivial information about their everyday lives preserved.

What then is striking about Picasso is the degree of attention given to the most minute details of his life. In one year, when Picasso was seventy-five, David Duncan took more than ten thousand photographs of him, scenes from three months of "every waking hour of every day."[3] Like Charlie Chaplin, whom he admired and once met, Picasso is the one visual artist who attracted the kind of attention given to genuinely famous people. In the 1950s Picasso led the life of a movie star, idolized by people who hardly knew anything of his artistic achievement. No earlier painter lived in such a public way; nor have any of his successors achieved anything like his fame.

How varied, Margot and Rudolf Wittkower's survey shows, are the lives of artists.[4] There are violent and gentle ones; painters and sculptors who became very rich, and many extremely poor; promiscuous artists, but also monogamous and even celibate ones. A few artists have been learned; many were entirely unintellectual. Even within the Baroque, an era richly endowed with singular personalities, the contrast between worldly figures like Bernini and Rubens and such very different men as Guido Reni, Poussin, and Vermeer points to the extreme difficulty of generalizing about artistic personalities.

Pablo Picasso became the richest serious painter in part because he was a beneficiary of the newly international art market.[5] He became much better known than any of his famed predecessors because of novel mass media not available to Leonardo, Rembrandt, or Manet. Of his near contemporaries, Mondrian and Giacometti were, in different ways, more strikingly radical; Matisse, more consistent, appears to have been as single-minded in his pursuit of financial success, but neither they nor any other more recent figures led a life remotely like Picasso's. The posthumous fascination with Pollock's life, and the recent literature on de Kooning's private affairs, feels intrusive; it remains external to their art. Jasper Johns attracts gossip, but neither he nor any of his contemporaries has become a celebrity. In comparison with Picasso, such famous painters as Brice Marden or Robert Ryman remain essentially private persons, almost unknown outside of the Manhattan art world.

With many artists, access to personal information seems beside the point. A recent detailed close-up biography of Mark Rothko provides fascinating details that remain difficult, still, to connect with his art. However much we learn about Rothko's childhood, his marriages, and his financial affairs, it isn't clear what plausible connection there could be between his painting and such a life. But with Picasso, what Eugene V. Thaw calls "the visual fact of the paintings themselves" is best understood by grasping the importance of role-playing in his life.[6] We can best answer Thaw's questions, "What do they look like?" and "How are they close to, or different from, other paintings in their tradition?" by using such information. Picasso lived the kind of life he chose, I believe, because he knew, perhaps consciously, that an audience's response was essential for interpretation of his work. This is why the gossipy commentator-friends— Françoise Gilot, James Lord, Patrick O'Brian, Fernande Olivier, Hélène Parmelin, Roland Penrose, Jaime Sabartès, and of course especially Richardson—reveal as much for my purposes as the more serious-seeming art historians.

In our age of gossip, when the personal life of anyone famous—athlete, politician, even poet—becomes the pretext for newspaper articles and, soon enough, books, it is not surprising that every well-known visual artist is also written about in these ways, as from early on Picasso was. The titles of books by people close to him—Olivier's *Picasso and His Friends*, Sabartès's *Picasso, an Intimate Portrait*, Gilot's *Life with Picasso*—naturally suggest a conception developed in one art-historical account, Mary Gedo's *Picasso: Art as Autobiography*, and frequently presented in both the art-historical and popular literature: extensive gossip about Picasso deserves to be so presented because his creative work is essentially autobiographical. He depicted in his paintings, sculptures, and prints the friends, lovers, and everyday objects surrounding him. In an often quoted statement from December 6, 1943, he said:

> Why do you think I date everything I do? Because it is not sufficient to know
> an artist's works—it is also necessary to know when he did them, why, how,
> under what circumstances. . . . Some day there will undoubtedly be a science
> . . . which will seek to learn more about man in general through the study of
> the creative man. . . . I want to leave to posterity a documentation that will be
> as complete as possible.[7]

When Olivier and Gilot incurred Picasso's wrath by publishing their accounts of his private life, they understood the spirit of his work, even though their writings were perceived by him as invasions of his privacy. Anyone who knows how readily significant errors occur in taped interviews will wonder about the accuracy of the published account of Picasso's conversations, some transcribed years, even decades, after the fact. "I'm not always quoted correctly," he said: "Besides, sometimes I'm forced to say things I don't mean."[8] And yet, although there is real need to be skeptical about the details of such accounts, this mass of evidence needs to be taken seriously. I place most trust in these records when they overlap, converging on common themes.

What better way to understand his achievement, then, than by gathering as much personal information as possible? This claim is so intuitively plausible that its denial deserves critical examination when such otherwise different distinguished Picasso scholars as Thaw and Rosalind E. Krauss react violently against it. Correctly linking this way of thinking about Picasso to a general preoccupation with art-as-autobiography—one of his targets is biographical Pollock commentary—Thaw argues:

> The most important evidence which confronts us is the visual fact of the
> paintings themselves. . . . Whatever they denote of the artist's psychological
> state is a subsidiary cause of their being and one of the less productive lines

FIGURE 2
**EL GRECO AND REMBRANDT
SURROUNDED BY PORTRAITS**
(cat. 53.6)
April 15, 17–19, 1968
Aquatint, scraper, and drypoint
From *Suite 347*

of inquiry because it can only be guesswork.[9]

Faced with Pollock's great late 1940s paintings, to cite an example Thaw discusses, it is very difficult to imagine in what ways biographical information enters into these abstractions. But when Picasso depicted men he admired, or women whom he loved or was coming to hate, personal information is no more irrelevant to "the visual facts" than is his view of politics irrelevant to *Guernica*. What is required is an account of how the artist's life enters into his paintings themselves. No doubt some guesswork is required, but the same is true with connoisseurship or any form of art-historical analysis.

Krauss, objecting to "an art history turned militantly away from all that is transpersonal in history—style, social and economic context, archive, structure," offers an argument based on her reading of the literature of analytic philosophy dealing with a major concern of that discipline, proper names.[10] Such a name, in her summary of material well known to philosophers, "has a referent but no sense." She thinks—and here she links this analytic tradition to the poststructuralist argumentation of Foucault and Barthes—that identifying a real person as "the 'key' to the image, and thus the 'meaning' of the image" cannot be the whole, or the only story.[11] Identifying Picasso's friend Casagemas as the figure depicted in *La Vie* (1904), for example, leaves out "the fact that the work is located in a highly fluctuating and ambiguous space of multiple planes of representation."

I admire her bravery in tackling this difficult tradition, which she misunderstands entirely. Analytic philosophers, unlike Foucault or Barthes, tried to analyze commonplace ways of speaking; uninterested in art, they were not dealing with pictorial reference. This argumentation of Frege, Russell, and Wittgenstein has in no way any direct application to analysis of visual artworks. Asserting that Picasso's paintings can only be understood in terms of social history, or economics, or style, and should be interpreted without any reference to his private life is entirely consistent with Frege's theorizing; so too is its denial. Analytic philosophers' answers to Frege's question, "How does the name 'Caesar' refer to Caesar?" tell nothing, and can tell nothing, about how we can explain visual artifacts.[12]

These obvious criticisms are mere picayune details, for certainly Thaw and Krauss are correct about the larger point: mere gathering of biographical details cannot in itself be the entire goal, not until or unless there is understanding of what to do with that information. Identifying figures depicted by Picasso with people associated with him cannot resolve the interpretative problems. Leo Steinberg's remarks about Richardson's account of *Les Demoiselles d'Avignon* points to the problems inherent in such approaches. Richardson argues that El Greco's *Apocalyptic Vision* (1608–14) is a key source; Steinberg replies that "to my eye the comparisons that give rise to such claims for influence or inspiration are rarely close enough to convince."[13] When dealing with the sources of such a much discussed picture by an often-interviewed artist, this disagreement is striking. However much information Richardson provides, drawing on his long-term relationship with the artist, what evidence could settle such a dispute? *Les Demoiselles* and

Apocalyptic Vision are visually similar, and Picasso knew this El Greco painting; who then is to say if it "influenced" his composition?

In seeking to satisfy "both the impulse of erotic possession and, at the same time, the most systematic investigation of the plane surface as a receptacle of information," Picasso—so Steinberg argues—"has had neither help nor companionship; nothing in modern art that encouraged it."[14] This is consistent, still, with acknowledging that such an investigation could only take place within the very special social setting created by that artist. Gilot describes her lover in a way that in this context is deeply revealing:

> All his life Pablo had identified . . . his role—even his fate—with that of certain
> other solitary performers: the anonymous acrobats and tumblers whom he
> etched so poignantly . . . the matadors whose struggles he made his own and
> whose drama, whose technique even, seemed to carry over into almost every
> phase of life and work.[15]

A performer needs an audience, for without spectators to whom he plays his actions will be meaningless; what must be shared if a performance is to come off is the belief that the performer's role is, within the confines of the play, real enough seeming to inspire confidence.

Other commentators draw attention to the relationship between the content of the early pictures showing *commedia dell'arte* figures and Picasso's later art. In Cubism, Michael Baxandall suggests, "the earlier narrative themes were appropriated by Picasso's own performance: what he had formerly depicted on the canvas he now enacted on the canvas as an acrobatic post-dramatic, occasionally joky 'mediation' on his own perceptual processes."[16]

Without appeal to close visual analysis, James Lord reaches a similar conclusion about Picasso's late lifestyle:

> In a tortuous way his life and work had come full circle. At the outset of his
> career he had liked to depict circus folk, equilibrists, and harlequins, and now

his work once more abounded in circus imagery, while the world press was filled with photographs of the eighty-year-old artist . . . playing the clown. His private life had, in fact, become a public circus.[17]

And Thaw himself says: "Picasso . . . is performing in the theater of the eye itself and he cavorts like a dazzling acrobat defying gravity."[18]

In his art, as in his life, his close associate Sabartès notes, Picasso performed. "His mind moves so rapidly from one thing to another that heaven and earth could not contain him or force him back . . . he changes the entire character of the theme, as he might a line when he sets about juggling it to shape one of his myriad fantasies."[19] For Alfred H. Barr, "the Blue period, with its . . . wistful acrobats . . . all this cumulative achievement was, so far as the main highway of modern painting was concerned, a personal and private bypath."[20] I think this is mistaken: judging these paintings thus fails to identify fully their place in Picasso's development.

After viewing the movie of Picasso working, Lord said: "It had been right and inevitable for Picasso to become fascinated by what he saw, for at every instant he had been actor, spectator, designer, director, producer, and proprietor in the theater of himself, which was the world stage."[21] The world as a theater is a very traditional theme. The title of Gert Schiff's essay on the late work, "The Musketeer and His *Theatrum Mundi*," makes explicit the archaic quality of Picasso's way of thinking.[22] Sixteenth- and 17th-century masques were centered on the king, whose power was defined by his place at the center.[23] When Picasso said, "painting isn't an aesthetic operation; it's a form of magic," he had this tradition in mind.[24] He was not talking about art as illusion, about the ways in which representations themselves are magical; he was describing this theatrical way of thinking. As Lord indicates, being drawn by Picasso seemed to give him, the artist's subject, a new identity. "The magic of the effect was too overwhelming. Where there had been nothing, suddenly there was being, of which I was possessed."[25]

FIGURE 3
**AT THE CIRCUS:
ACROBATS, GIRAFFE,
SWIMMERS. . .**
(cat. 53.4)
April 11, 1968
Etching
From *Suite 347*

FIGURE 4
**PICASSO THE
TOURIST RETURNS
TO THE FOUNTAIN
OF CANALETAS**
(cat. 53.12)
May 13, 1968
Etching
From *Suite 347*

How did Picasso learn to fashion his life thus? When young he knew Punch-and-Judy shows.[26] Later he worked with Jean Cocteau for the ballet; and he loved the circus, a love—Brassaï reports—his wife Olga and son found incomprehensible. "The circus was a link with his past . . . all over the Spain of his childhood hereditary troupes of tumblers were to be seen, sometimes leading apes or bears; and fire-eaters, sword-swallowers, and mountebanks were common at the fairs."[27] His son with Gilot was named Claude, she reports, because she thought of Watteau's teacher, Claude Gillot, who did many paintings of harlequins.[28] And certainly his fascination with bullfights is relevant.

Perhaps he learned something when in the scene described by Olivier, he and Apollinaire found themselves trying to dispose of the stolen Louvre sculptures: "I am sure that without realizing it they were seeing themselves as characters in a play . . . they had, during the agonizing hours of waiting . . . pretended to play cards, like gangsters."[29] Certainly he learned from his negotiations with dealers, as Gilot reports:

> Sometimes he would have us act out little playlets which prepared the routine of the next day. . . . Sometimes Pablo kept his own role and I would take the part of the dealer, or I would be Pablo and Pablo would be the dealer. . . . If I answered something which wasn't in character, Pablo would correct me and I had to find something else. . . . He had the last word because he had more wit, more fantasy, more imagination, more arms of all kinds, than his opponent.[30]

Parmelin makes similar observations about his discussion style:

> One should never try to be in the right when arguing with Picasso. For even if one is right, one is wrong, since it is utterly impossible to demonstrate one's correctness to him, not to give up first, and not to avoid the red herrings he drags across one's line of reasoning. One may be right, but the Minotaur devours one.[31]

Performing was a way for Picasso to identify himself with those masters on whose work he did variations:

> The artist used a slide machine to project "The Night Watch" . . . on his studio wall—thus enabling the musketeers to step straight out of seventeenth-century Amsterdam into the time-warp of Picasso's *teatrum mundi*.[32]

Then "the old masters are always there, and the proof is that Picasso can bring them and their painting back to life. The theater he creates is there for just this purpose."[33]

Still, all of this information does not explain how Picasso came to fashion his life very self-consciously, creating in his houses a small-scale court society. Other artists did ballet sets, enjoyed popular entertainments, quoted the old masters, and manipulated their dealers without coming also to play their everyday lives in these self-consciously theatrical ways. Picasso, I think, needed his wonderfully willful, often entertaining, no doubt sometimes merely stupid social life, for it was one source for and support of his art. Depicting such scenes when very young, when he was still a nobody, he learned to play these roles in reality. His art making took place not just in the studio, where usually he was alone, but also in the waiting rooms in which he socialized with his courtiers, hangers-on who, far from being mere extras, were essential to his conception of himself, and so therefore also to his art. The ultimate absolute value of his work remains, still, to be determined. As performer, he remains without rival.

Only one artist is comparable to Picasso in the way he chose to be presented, and in the attention he drew to his personal life, the man who once expressed the desire to be either Picasso or (how characteristic!) the Queen of England. The self-evident analogy between the social process of art making in Andy Warhol's Factory and Picasso's studio life and the obvious parallels between the reporting of minutia in Bob Colacello's book *Holly Terror: Andy Warhol Close-Up* and the lives of Picasso by his intimates are striking. So too are the obvious differences between a man who, so the great student of urban life Richard Sennett told me, loved to watch self-destructive people, and Picasso. These differences are nicely condensed in the contrast between *Bull's Head* (1943) and Warhol's semi-readymade, *Brillo Box* (1964). Picasso's goal, Penrose explains, was to make "a magical transformation from an insignificant piece of scrap to a creature endowed with the nervous tension of life."[34] This Ovidian concern with metamorphosis, Picasso's fascination with changing an industrial artifact into what appears to be a living thing, has an interesting relationship to Warhol's glamorizing of a banal industrial object by nudging it into the art world. Picasso was fascinated, Parmelin tells, to think how this transformation could be reversed:

> One day I took the seat and the handlebars, I put one on top of the other
> and I made a bull's head. Well and good. But what I should have done was
> to throw away the bull's head. . . . Then a worker would have passed by.
> He'd have picked it up. And he'd have found that, perhaps, he could
> have made a bicycle seat and handlebars with that bull's head. . . . That's
> the gift of metamorphosis.[35]

In his account of *Les Demoiselles d'Avignon*, Leo Steinberg draws attention to the way in which that painting achieves its proper unity only when the spectator's presence is taken into account:

> In the *Demoiselles* . . . no two figures maintain the kind of mutual rapport that
> excludes us; and the three central figures address the observer with unsparing
> directness. . . . The shift is away from narrative and objective action to an
> experience centered in the beholder. The work . . . is not a self-existent
> abstraction, since the solicited viewer is a constituent factor.[36]

Or, as he says briefly in an earlier essay: "Everyone can see that the ladies are having company."[37] Might we not better understand the body of Picasso's work by generalizing these observations? Unifying Steinberg's essays "Picasso's Sleepwatchers" (1968) and "The Algerian Women and Picasso at Large" (1972) with this more recent commentary is this concern with the spectator's role.

FIGURE 5
THEATER: AROUND REMBRANDT (cat. 53.16)
May 25, 1968
Aquatint and sugar lift
From *Suite 347*

In proposing this reading of Picasso's career I am only extending this analysis. All the information I present is available already in the literature, but it has not been synthesized in this, my way.

"Whoever needs somebody else is necessitous and so takes up a position."[38] In this view of life as playacting—presented in Denis Diderot's *Rameau's Nephew*, commented on with great fascination by Hegel, and then presented in a sociological context in the 1950s by Erving Goffman—the self is defined by, and perhaps even coextensive with, a set of roles, as if the world of everyday life were but a theater:

> On the stage one player presents himself in the guise of a character to char-
> acters projected by other players; the audience constitutes a third party. . . . In
> real life, the three parties are compressed into two; the part one individual
> plays is tailored to the parts played by the others present, and yet these others
> also constitute the audience.[39]

Whatever the general truth of this general way of thinking, whose far-reaching philosophical implications are difficult to evaluate, it is a useful way of identifying Picasso's goals.

"Painting isn't an aesthetic operation," Gilot reports Picasso having said; "it's a form of magic."[40] Speaking of magic can easily seem reactionary or seriously unanalytical. "The essence of magic is the primitive belief that the will can control the latent forces and spirits residing in all objects and all nature": John Berger misses the point here, and so analyzing his error helps explain Picasso's personality.[41] Taking magic literally in an era of modernist technology and positivistic philosophy would, I grant, be regressive. But in speaking of "magic" I am concerned not only and not just with primitive prescientific development, but with what Freud identified in the account of his grandson's "fort-da" (here-there) play, as the child's attempt to keep present his mother. That play, the source of Freud's very rationalistic analysis of the death instinct, is one source of the account of symbols in "Meditations on a Hobby Horse," the Freudian account of

FIGURE 6
**FANTASY OF THE GENRE OF
FÜSSLI'S "NIGHTMARE," WITH
A VOYEUR UNDER THE BED**
(cat. 53.9)
April 28, 1968
Etching and drypoint
From *Suite 347*

Sir Ernst Gombrich; and also the basis of what we all experience in the theater or at the movies. "Magic," as I use that word, takes place within the confines of the theatrical performance, where such playacting comes off, even as the performer and his audience know that they are only engaged in a form of play.

Many Picasso commentators moralize about him, in terms that reveal a striking lack of feeling for this aspect of his career.[42] If only, Berger writes, Picasso—like Lenin, Berger's onetime hero—had come to terms with modern times:

> Picasso should have left Europe, to which he has never properly belonged . . .
> seeking for his unique people in whose name he might speak. He might have
> visited India, Indonesia, China, Mexico or West Africa.[43]

As if it were likely that this stay-at-home, who only at Cocteau's instigation went as far from Paris as Rome, might have become a world traveler, a rich visitor to be hosted by the local communist

FIGURE 7
**MEMORIES: CIRCUS WITH "THE GIANT"
AND SELF-PORTRAIT AS BABY-OLD MAN**
(cat. 53.20)
June 4, 1968
Aquatint, etching, and scraper used as drypoint
From *Suite 347*

parties. Or, as an even less happily prophetic Russian commentator wrote in 1926: "If he were to live and work in our country, his talent might develop even more comprehensively and extend to fields that are new even to him."[44]

The trouble with Picasso, Mary Gedo opines, is that "he both chose inappropriate female partners, and then could never definitely sever his ties to these women once they lost interest in him."[45] How odd that a psychoanalyst should judge that the loves of an aggressively decisive man were not true to his desires. "In such a matter," Patrick O'Brian more plausibly writes, "the springs of a man's conduct are . . . so deeply hidden that speculation is not only impertinent but useless."[46] Picasso, mostly a failure as a father and a difficult husband, made art that is so bound up with his life that there is an air of absurdity in admiring his work and imagining him living in more "mature" ways. "He took to its ultimate conclusion the negative vision of the modernist world," Arianna Huffington writes, "he was in fact a time-bound genius, a seismograph for the conflicts, turmoil and anguish of his age."[47] Were that true, and it seems to me mistaken to define modernism in terms of negativity, then how can he be criticized as she does? Why make Picasso, rather than Brecht, Corbusier, or Schoenberg the seismograph of his era? In truth, he was only another painter. I place more faith in Lord's remarks about "how perverse, cruel, ruthless, sentimental, and promiscuous Picasso could be . . . how could anyone honestly study his work and imagine him to be otherwise?" It also is important, Lord adds, "to know that upon occasion no one could be more charming, witty, incisive, magnetic, responsive and generous."[48]

In his essay "Art and Disturbation," Arthur C. Danto, writing about Nietzsche's theory of Dionysian rituals and their connection with modern performance art, discusses the relationship of art with magic:

> The disturbatory artist aims to transform her audience into something pretheatrical, a body which relates to her in some more magical and transformational relationship than the defining conventions of the theater

allow . . . she means to achieve this by some transformation of herself, which

consists in taking off the protective and powerfully dislocative atmosphere of

theatrical distance and making contact with a reality.[49]

In the theater, normally the audience remains at an aesthetic distance from the events on stage, set apart from the actors. In disturbatory art, the barriers between actor and audience come down. Such performances are thus like role-playing in everyday life, as described by Goffman, where "if a performance is to come off, the witnesses by and large must be able to believe that the performers are sincere."[50] This primitive conception of art is difficult, Danto goes on to suggest, to recreate today. In our art world, the iconoclast's nightmare, that a representation manifest the god's real presence, that it be a totem and not simply remain a mere representation, has come to seem essentially unthinkable.[51] (Outside fundamentalist cultures, erotic art alone now retains such primitive power.) In so far as making *Les Demoiselles d'Avignon* was, as André Malraux reports, an act of exorcism for its creator, that private ritual today is only a subject for scholarly reconstruction. "I do not enjoy disturbatory art," Danto says in a passage that expresses, also, my view, "perhaps because I am always outside it and see it as pathetic and futile."[52]

But in one very interesting way, Picasso was a disturbatory artist, a great modern master of performance art. His conception of how to organize his life and organize commentary on his work is essentially Nietzschian. The chorus, *The Birth of Tragedy* explains, is

the mirror image in which the Dionysian man contemplates himself. This

phenomenon is best made clear by imagining an actor who, being truly

talented, sees the role he is supposed to play quite palpably before his eyes.

The satyr chorus is, first of all, a vision of the Dionysian mass of spectators,

just as the world of stage, in turn, is a vision of this satyr chorus. . . . In this

magic transformation the Dionysian reveler sees himself as a satyr, *and as a*

satyr, in turn, he sees the god.[53]

What the spectators see, Nietzsche adds, is not "the awkwardly masked human being but rather a visionary figure, born as it were from their own rapture." Or, as Peter Schjeldhal writes in an instructive review which, without mentioning Nietzsche, shows the ongoing relevance of this way of thinking: "Any art, when it works, forms a fleeting community, a oneness with imagined others in pledging allegiance to something."[54]

What his familiars saw in Picasso's studio, I am suggesting, was not the truly gifted actor, who by turns was generous, manipulative, and off-putting, but something like this vision of Dionysus; they viewed Picasso-the-performance-artist. What Picasso saw in turn was not merely those hangers-on, a few of them intellectuals or artists, some art dealers, many just hustlers or spectators attracted by the prospect of seeing a celebrity. No: what he saw as he acted was a mirror in which his illusionistically real presence as Dionysian performer was revealed. In such a situation, "the artist as artist is a performer, a purveyor of expressiveness, and so his experience is theatrical."[55] Is it surprising that often Picasso's audience was undemanding? A life-long beach goer who never learnt to swim, he thrashed about in the sea, playacting that fooled even some of his biographers. At a magician's show, when a performance is good, only a rationalist with a heart of stone would critically look closely at the performer.

Such role-playing was real fantasy that made Picasso's art possible. It is revealing to see what happened when a few people—some like James Lord's lover Bernard, now with no independent identity; others famous like Giacometti—refused to take part in Picasso's performances:

> Giacometti was one of the very few never overawed by Picasso, because the essential condition of his respect for others forbade the notion that any person should by virtue of no matter what attainment be the object of special consideration.[56]

Then, as happens in a theatrical performance so inept that it fails, or at mass for an unbeliever,

FIGURE 8
**OLD MAN THINKING OVER HIS LIFE: GALLANT
YOUTH, MATURITY AS A FAMOUS PAINTER,
WORK CREATED IN THE SLUMS NOW ENTHRONED
BENEATH A CANOPY** (cat. 53.18)
May 28, 1969
Sugar-lift aquatint
From *Suite 347*

the "magic" ceases to work and so the performer—ceasing to be a character in the drama—remains only a mere actor.

In Baudelaire's prose poem "Une Mort héroïque," the jester dies because he crosses the line between performance and so-called real life. It is natural to become confused about that border line; when engrossed in a performance, can the actor remember, always, that he is only playing a game? Some artists and intellectuals who engage, knowingly or not, in role-playing end up unable to tell appearance from reality, confusing mere art and real life. For all of his role-playing, Picasso had a good robust sense of reality. "In art Picasso was a hero, less so in life." Neither hero nor villain, for as Richardson adds, "an obsessive concern with self-preservation was one of his most consistent characteristics."[57] Picasso was not subsumed in his roles. "Picasso always likes," Sabartès says, "to keep to himself a part of what he thinks. One might imagine that he confesses everything—but far from it!"[58] But what he was in himself, as opposed to how he was when he performed for others?

I am uncertain that there is any answer to this question for it is unclear to me if he ever really stopped performing. Steinberg argues that at life's end,

> it is as if the potent personae that had served through seventy years to parade his self-image—as harlequin, lover, ravisher, bull, minotaur, monster, artist-creator, or virtuoso performer—it is as if these had been no more than aspects presented to hosts of admirers . . . as if all these roles, like all aspects whatsoever, had been staged masquerades, spectacles, circus routines—marvelously diverting and partly revealing, yet still misting over a reservoir of dank, sunken feeling.[59]

Faced with death Picasso became sincere, revealing what he had done earlier to be mere playacting. This of course is a familiar way of thinking about role-playing. Beneath the protean performer lies some authentic self; behind the play of appearances, we find true reality. "How

tiresome always to be pretending," the performer whispers in an aside to his close friend; "thank heavens that I can tell you alone the whole truth." At the end of a text, after all the alternatives have been weighed, what we expect and normally get is the author's own position. What better time, analogously, for Picasso to lay aside his roles than at the end of a long life?

From the writer's perspective, sincere, plain straight speaking can be but another trope, like writing to a friend, telling him in private what could not be said in public. The hard-to-answer query, still, is whether role-playing can be entirely escaped. Must Picasso in the home stretch become the Picasso revealing his real self? Looking at the mysterious untitled etching with aquatint from February 3 and March 5 and 6, 1970, which sets a stage scene with performers in a field of observers who also engage in independent action, I am aware of what Steinberg stresses, the difficulty of understanding, or even identifying Picasso's thought processes in his last years. One reason he is a very deep artist is that he inspires commentary on these perhaps unanswerable questions.

I owe the central idea for this essay to street performers in Frankfurt who on a hot July 1995 evening entertained a large crowd, including me and my family eating dinner out-of-doors before we went to visit a museum. For a magical moment, we were caught up in their world of playacting. Fascinated by such archaic role-playing, I never even learned these performers' names and gave them what, looking back, seems far too little money when after the show was over they came to our table. I owe them a lot, but how was I to know then that they would provide me with the key to understanding the art and life of Pablo Picasso?[60]

In thanks for their contributions to Picasso scholarship, and their support for my writing, I dedicate this essay to Richard Shone and Arne Glimcher.

COLOR PLATES

COLOR PLATE 1
HEAD OF A WOMAN, NO. 3 (PORTRAIT OF DORA MAAR) (cat. 13.1)
January–June 1939
Aquatint and scraper

COMPOSITION WITH VASE OF FLOWERS (cat. 22)
March 10, 1947
Lithograph printed in three colors

COLOR PLATE 3
WOMAN WITH HAIRNET (cat. 37)
September 1956
Lithograph printed in four colors

COLOR PLATE 4
"PORTRAIT OF A YOUNG WOMAN"
(AFTER LUCAS CRANACH THE YOUNGER). II (cat. 42)
July 4, 1958
Linocut printed in five colors

COLOR PLATE 5
STILL LIFE WITH GLASS UNDER THE LAMP (cat. 52)
March 19, 1962
Linocut printed in four colors

COLOR PLATE 6
PICADOR AND BULL (cat. 45)
September 5–6, 1959
Linocut printed in four colors

COLOR PLATE 7
PICADOR AND BULL (cat. 44)
August 30, 1959
Linocut printed in three colors

COLOR PLATE 8
BACCHANAL WITH YOUNG GOAT AND ONLOOKER (cat. 47)
November 27, 1959
Linocut printed in five colors

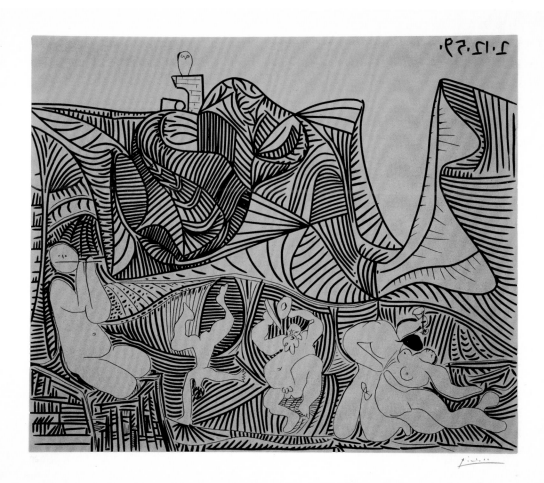

COLOR PLATE 9
BACCHANAL WITH OWL (cat. 48)
December 2, 1959
Linocut printed in two colors

COLOR PLATE 10
LARGE HEAD OF A WOMAN IN A HAT (cat. 51)
February 9, 1962
Linocut printed in four colors

COLOR PLATE 11
HEAD OF FAUN (cat. 50)
February 7, 1962
Linocut printed in two colors

COLOR PLATE 12
PORTRAIT OF JACQUELINE LEANING ON HER ELBOWS (cat. 46)
October 2, 1959
Linocut printed in two colors

CATALOGUE OF THE EXHIBITION

CATALOGUE OF THE EXHIBITION

BETSY G. FRYBERGER

NOTES ON CATALOGUE ENTRIES

REFERENCES

Information in the catalogue entries is based on two catalogues raisonnés: one by Brigitte Baer of intaglio prints and linocuts, the other by Fernand Mourlot of lithographs (see Bibliography). Prints are listed in chronological order, following either Baer or Mourlot (the English and French editions of the latter have the same numbering, but the later English edition has some additional information). Other citations include Georges Bloch's catalogue of prints and the Galerie Louise Leiris numbers for *Suite 347*.

TITLES AND DATES

Entries on intaglio and linocut prints incorporate Baer's extensive research with new titles and redating. English translations are based on Baer's French titles. Where there is little or no difference between the French and English titles, only the English are cited. Book or portfolio titles are given in capitals to differentiate them from single published prints. (Since Baer used capital Roman numerals to indicate states, we have followed that form for the intaglio prints and linocuts. However, since Mourlot described the lithographs with the more usual lower case, we have followed that style for those prints.)

SERIES AND STATES

Prints from series are grouped under a single number, as in the *Suite Vollard*, although a year or more may intervene between prints. Plate numbers, when given, follow references to Baer or Mourlot, and Bloch. Progressive states of lithographs are grouped under a single main number. If information about papers, watermarks, signatures, and inscriptions is consistent within these groups or series, it is cited only once.

TECHNIQUES

Etchings, drypoints, and aquatints are printed from copperplates, unless noted. All intaglio prints published by Ambroise Vollard, Daniel-Henry Kahnweiler, and Galerie Louise Leiris were printed from steel-faced plates, unless noted. Descriptions of intaglio and linocut techniques may abbreviate those as cited in Baer. Lithographs are described as being drawn on either stone or zinc, with a brief description of the technique—crayon, pen, wash—roughly in the sequence used, based on Mourlot's catalogue, but again sometimes in shortened form. Details of transfer techniques are not given. Lithographs are printed in black except as noted.

PHYSICAL DESCRIPTION

Measurements are metric; height precedes width. For intaglio prints the plate dimensions are given; for lithographs those of the composition.

PRINTERS AND PUBLISHERS

All lithographs were printed at the Mourlot workshop and published by the Galerie Louise Leiris. All linocuts were printed at Hidalgo Arnéra's workshop and were also published by the Galerie Louise Leiris. Intaglio prints of the 1960s were published by Galerie Louise Leiris.

INSCRIPTIONS

When an impression is signed, annotated, and numbered, that information is given. If the work is signed in colored inks or crayons, that is noted; otherwise all signatures are in pencil. Impressions from the groups of 5 or 18 proofs reserved for the artist are neither signed nor numbered.

PROVENANCE

One hundred and sixty-eight *bon à tirer* proofs and sixty proofs reserved for the artist came from the collection of Fernand Mourlot, as well as seven proofs dedicated to him, in the 1977 purchase of 228 lithographs. The Mourlot provenance is not noted individually in the catalogue entries. Two impressions, formerly in the collection of Marie-Thérèse Walter, however, are noted.

1. CIRCUS PERFORMERS

Les Saltimbanques
1913, Paris
Published by Ambroise Vollard
Printed by Louis Fort on Van
Gelder wove paper in an
edition of 250

The following two drypoints
were included in the group of
fourteen published by Vollard
in 1913.

1.1

1.1 CIRCUS PERFORMERS

Les Saltimbanques
1905, spring–summer, Paris
Drypoint
28.8 x 33.0 cm
Stamped: *Picasso 1905*
Baer 9 II.b.2; Bloch 7

1.2 SALOME

1905, summer–end of the year,
Paris
Drypoint
40.3 x 34.6 cm
Baer 17 III.b.2; Bloch 14

1.2

2. SAINT MATOREL

by Max Jacob, 1911, Paris
Published by Daniel-Henry Kahnweiler
Book with 4 etchings
Printed by Eugène Delâtre on
Van Gelder laid paper
Signed by Max Jacob and Picasso on
the colophon
Numbered: 23 (of 100)

One of the first books illustrated
with Cubist prints, *Saint Matorel*
is part of a trilogy. This is the first
volume, the second was illustrated
by André Derain, the third again
by Picasso; all were published by
Kahnweiler. The protagonist is an
ordinary Parisian, Victor Matorel; his
friend is Mlle Léonie. After a debate
in a convent in Barcelona, Matorel
undergoes a mystical conversion;
Jacob had converted to Catholicism.

2.1 MLLE LEONIE ON A CHAISE LONGUE

Mlle Léonie sur une chaise longue
1910, summer, Cadaquès or Paris
Etching, scraper, and drypoint
19.8 x 14.1 cm
Baer 25 IV.b.3; Bloch 21

2.2 THE CONVENT (SECOND PLATE)

Le Couvent (Deuxième Planche)
1910, August, Cadaquès
Etching
20.0 x 14.2 cm
Baer 26 b.3; Bloch 22

2.1

2.2

3. HEAD OF MAN WITH PIPE

Tête d'homme à la pipe
1911?, or more probably 1912,
spring, Paris
Etching
13.0 x 11.0 cm
Signed proof printed by Delâtre
on Arches laid paper
Baer 32 b; Bloch 23

4. STILL LIFE WITH BOTTLE
OF MARC

Nature morte à la bouteille de marc
1911, August, Ceret, or autumn, Paris
Drypoint
49.9 x 30.5 cm
Published by D.-H. Kahnweiler
Printed 1912 by Delâtre on Arches laid
paper
Signed and numbered: *23/100*
Baer 33 b; Bloch 24

I. ETCHINGS,
1930-1940

In Picasso's first extended printmaking statement Vollard played a pivotal role, commissioning and publishing book illustrations and the major suite that bears his name. Vollard, although primarily an art dealer, published many original prints and helped create the new form of *livre d'artiste*. Starting in the 1890s, working with the master lithographer Auguste Clot, he published portfolios of color lithographs by Bonnard, Vuillard, and Roussel, as well as several sets by Redon in extraordinarily subtle gradations of black. By the early 20th century his *livres d'artistes* were designed with distinction, using elegant typography and printed on fine handmade papers, in collaboration with designers, master printers, and artists from Picasso to Matisse and Rouault.

When Vollard approached Picasso with the project of illustrating Balzac's *Chef-d'oeuvre inconnu*, about a reclusive artist and his unknown masterpiece, Picasso responded to the heart of the story, but ignored its narrative. Instead, his etchings of 1927–28 focus on the artist at work and the relationship between artist and model. At times the model is tall and young, at another she is heavy and middle-aged—more concierge than model—as she sits and knits; another scene shows a model scrutinizing the artist's work (cats. 5.1–5.3). The second book project, begun in 1930, was suggested by Albert Skira. These illustrations based on Ovid's *Métamorphoses* appealed to Picasso because of the many tales of transformation.

The major publication of the decade was the suite of one hundred prints known as *Suite Vollard*. In execution the etchings span the decade of the 1930s, but only a few date from the opening or closing years; most are concentrated in the two-year period, 1933–34, when Picasso was working on sculpture at Boisgeloup. The first plate, executed in a simple line etching, continues the cool classicizing line of the Ovid illustrations; the closing plate, executed in aquatint, is a portrait of Vollard (cat. 8.21). The etchings published in the *Suite Vollard* constitute Picasso's major printmaking activity of the 1930s. Included are most of his fully realized works and the level of technical complexity attained new subtlety in the later prints when he began to work with a new printer and explored tonal nuances. Norton Simon purchased the complete sets of illustrations for Balzac and Ovid in 1968 and the *Suite Vollard* in 1969.

5. LE CHEF-D'OEUVRE INCONNU

The Unknown Masterpiece
by Honoré de Balzac, 1931, Paris
Published by Ambroise Vollard
Book with 13 etchings, 63 wood engravings
and 16 reproductions of Picasso's drawings
Printed by Louis Fort on BFK Rives wove
paper
Signed and numbered on the colophon: *XIV*
From the *hors commerce* edition of 35

5.1

Set in the early years of the 17th century in
Paris, where young Poussin has only recently
arrived, the story centers on his visit to the
studio of the established painter Pourbus at
7 rue des Grands-Augustins (where Picasso
later had a studio). The young painter
encounters the old artist Frenhofer, who tells
of working for ten years on a single painting
of a woman, which he has not shown anyone.
Poussin and Pourbus persuade Frenhofer to
let them see this work. When they do, the
canvas has been so painted over that it
appears only as a tangle of lines. Picasso's
etchings do not follow the details of the
narrative but rather concentrate on scenes
of the artist in his studio.

5.2

5.1 SCULPTOR IN FRONT OF HIS SCULPTURE, WITH A YOUNG WOMAN WEARING A TURBAN AND A SCULPTED HEAD
*Sculpteur devant sa sculpture, avec jeune
fille au turban et tête sculptée*
1927–28, Paris
Etching
19.3 x 27.8 cm
Baer 123 b.1*y*; Bloch 82

5.2 PAINTER AND MODEL KNITTING
Peintre et modèle tricotant
1927, Paris
Etching
19.4 x 27.8 cm
Baer 126 b.1*y*; Bloch 85

5.3 PAINTER AT WORK, WATCHED BY A NUDE MODEL
Peintre au travail, observé par un modèle nu
1927–28, Paris
Etching
19.3 x 27.7 cm
Baer 130 b.1*y*; Bloch 89

5.3

6. LES METAMORPHOSES

The Metamorphoses
by Ovid, 1931, Lausanne
Published by Albert Skira
Book with 30 etchings
Printed by Louis Fort on Arches
handmade laid paper
Inscribed by Picasso on title page:
Imprimé pour Léon Pichon
Not signed, but numbered on
the colophon: *XIV*
From the *hors commerce*
edition of 20

Gilmour, in her essay "Marie-
Thérèse: A Perfect Odalisque,"
discusses how frequently Walter,
Picasso's new love, appears in these
etchings. Picasso's illustrations for
Ovid's epic were drawn in long,
sinuous strokes. The adventures
and transformations of gods and
goddesses are distilled and distant.
Published the same year as Balzac's
Chef-d'oeuvre inconnu, Ovid's
Métamorphoses was the first book
Albert Skira published. Skira, whose
small office on rue La Boétie was
near Picasso's studio, presented the
first proofs to the artist on October
25, 1931, his fiftieth birthday.

6.1

6.1 FALL OF PHAETON AND THE CHARIOT OF THE SUN
Chute de Phaéton avec le char du soleil
September 20, 1930, Boisgeloup
Etching
22.5 x 17.0 cm
Baer 146 b.2.ß; Bloch 102

6.2 THREE FEMALE NUDES
Trois femmes nues
1931, early April?, Boisgeloup
Etching
13.8 x 16.8 cm
Baer 149 b.2.ß; Bloch 105

6.2

6.3

6.3 NESTOR RELATING THE STORY OF THE TROJAN WAR
Récits de Nestor sur la guerre de Troie
September 21, 1930, Boisgeloup
Etching
22.2 x 17.0 cm
Baer 166 b.2.ß; Bloch 122

7. THE DIVER   (illus. p. 62)
La Plongeuse
November 29, 1932, Paris
Etching printed over collage of sand- and salmon-colored papers
14.0 x 11.2 cm
Printed by Roger Lacourière in an edition of 100 on Arches wove paper
Signed
Baer 277 B.b; Bloch 1322

Cutting small pieces of colored papers (and other materials) into shapes, Picasso made different arrangements of them, which Lacourière and assistants printed in an edition of 100. (See Baer 277 for further details.) The unusually deeply etched lines appear lined with bubbles, reinforcing the reference to water. Gilmour discusses Walter as the drowning swimmer; see "Marie-Thérèse: A Perfect Odalisque."

8. SUITE VOLLARD

1939, Paris
Published by Ambroise Vollard
100 etchings, some with sugar-lift aquatint
Printed by Roger Lacourière on Montval
laid paper
From the edition of 50 with Montgolfier
watermark, except as noted
Signed

The numerical sequence given to the
plates when they were published does
not correspond to the order in which they
were completed. The prints are exhibited
here in their chronological sequence. Many
of the prints were made at Picasso's studio
at Boisgeloup outside Paris, where he was
working on his sculpture, making large
plaster heads of Marie-Thérèse Walter that
appear in several etchings (cats. 8.4 and 8.5).
The sequence begins with a placid seated
nude (cat. 8.1) who closely resembles the
Ovid figures, but in the next several
sequences new motifs are developed—
bullfights, *The Battle of Love* (cat. 8.7), and
Rembrandt. The longest sequence, which
runs to more than forty scenes, was created
mainly from March to May 1933, and in it
Picasso returned to the theme of the artist
in his studio. After opening with a sculptor
and model looking at a statue of a classical
male nude, the following scenes show a
sculptor at work on a plaster of Marie-
Thérèse Walter (cat. 8.4). The sculptor in
this sequence is characterized variously—
at times youthful or old, but mainly mature
and handsome, with a godlike head of curly
hair and beard, a reprise from Ovid (cat.
8.4). The sculptures depicted begin with a
large female head and a Surrealist torso
(cat. 8.8), but later several classical groups
are added—a horse and rider, a bull with a
nymph. The models change, Sarah Murphy
is paired with a premonition of Françoise
Gilot (cat. 8.12), then Ingres's odalisques
crowd the studio (cat. 8.13). A Minotaur
enters, and after drinking with the sculptor
and model, he takes on the role of the
sculptor. One of the most moving sequences
is of a Blind Minotaur, created in late
1934–35, with more layered iconography
(cats. 8.15–8.17). The series ends with three
portraits of Vollard made on a single day in
March 1937 (cat. 8.21).

8.1

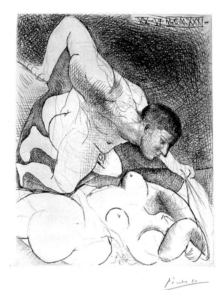

8.2

**8.1 SEATED NUDE CROWNED WITH
FLOWERS, LEGS CROSSED**
*Femme nue couronnée de fleurs,
aux jambes croisées*
September 16, 1930, Boisgeloup
Etching
22.6 x 17.2 cm
Baer 192 B.c; Bloch 134; SV Plate 1

8.2 MAN UNVEILING A WOMAN
(illus. p. 61)
Homme dévoilant une femme
June 20, 1931, Boisgeloup or Paris
Drypoint
29.3 x 36.5 cm
Baer 203 II.B.c; Bloch 138; SV Plate 5

8.3 SCULPTOR, MODEL, AND SCULPTURE, SEATED WOMAN

Sculpteur, modèle et sculpture: femme assise
March 15, 1933, Paris
Drypoint and scraper
31.8 x 18.4 cm
Baer 297 VI.B.c; Bloch 146; SV Plate 40

8.4 MODEL AND SCULPTOR WITH HIS SCULPTURE (illus. p. 10)

Modèle et sculpteur avec sa sculpture
March 17, 1933, Paris
Etching
26.0 x 18.9 cm
Baer 300 B.c; Bloch 148; SV Plate 38

8.5 TWO WOMEN LOOKING AT A SCULPTED HEAD (illus. p. 56)

Deux femmes regardant une tête sculptée
March 21, 1933, Paris
Etching
26.4 x 26.0 cm
Baer 302 B.c; Bloch 150; SV Plate 42

8.4

8.3

8.5

8.6 SCULPTOR AND HIS MODEL WITH A BUST ON A COLUMN

Sculpteur et son modèle avec un buste sur une colonne
March 31, 1933, Paris
Etching
19.0 x 26.5 cm
Baer 322 B.c; Bloch 169; SV Plate 60

8.7 COUPLING. I

Accouplement. I
November 2, 1933, Paris
Etching and drypoint
19.5 x 27.5 cm
Baer 340 II.B.c; Bloch 181; SV Plate 29

Two similar compositions date from April 1933, leading Bloch to conclude that this print was made at the same time; however, Baer has corrected the date to November 2.

8.8 MARIE-THERESE LOOKING AT HER EFFIGY AS A SURREALIST SCULPTURE

Marie-Thérèse considérant son effigie surréaliste sculptée
May 4, 1933, Paris
Etching
26.5 x 19.0 cm
Baer 346 B.c; Bloch 187; SV Plate 74

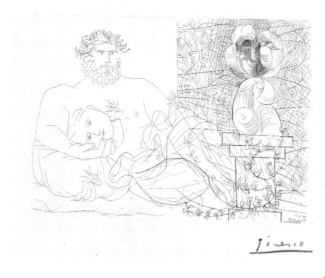

8.6

8.7

8.8

8.9

8.10

8.11

8.9 MARIE-THERESE, AS A VESTAL GUARDIAN, WATCHING OVER THE SLEEPING MINOTAUR

Marie-Thérèse en vestale, veillant le minotaure endormi
May 18, 1933, Paris
Etching
19.0 x 26.5 cm
Baer 352 III.B.c; Bloch 193; SV Plate 86

8.10 DYING MINOTAUR WITH COMPASSIONATE YOUNG WOMAN

Minotaure mourant et jeune femme pitoyable
May 30, 1933, Paris
Etching
19.0 x 26.5 cm
Baer 366 B.c; Bloch 198; SV Plate 90

8.11 MINOTAUR CARESSING THE HAND OF A SLEEPING WOMAN WITH HIS MUZZLE

(illus. p. 67)
Minotaure caressant du mufle la main d'une dormeuse
June 18, 1933, Boisgeloup, finished probably 1934
Drypoint
29.5 x 36.6 cm
Baer 369 II.B.c; Bloch 201; SV Plate 93

**8.12 AT THE BATH. WOMAN IN
FLOWERED HAT AND WOMAN
WRAPPED IN A TOWEL**
(illus. p. 65)
*Au bain. Femme au chapeau à fleurs et
femme drapée dans une serviette*
January 29, 1934, Paris
Etching
27.4 x 19.6 cm
Baer 408 B.c; Bloch 210; SV Plate 79

**8.13 FOUR WOMEN WITH SCULPTED
VOYEUR. (A NOD TO INGRES'S
"TURKISH BATH")**
*Femmes entre elles avec voyeur sculpté.
(Clin d'oeil au "Bain Turc' d'Ingres")*
March 10, 1934, and probably late 1934,
Paris
Etching, scraper, and burin
22.2 x 31.4 cm
Baer 424 V.B.c; Bloch 219; SV Plate 82

**8.14 MARIE-THERESE AS A
WOMAN BULLFIGHTER** (illus. p. 1)
Marie-Thérèse en femme torero
June 20, 1934, Paris
Etching
29.7 x 23.7 cm
Signed and numbered in red ink: *9/15*
Baer 426 B.c; Bloch 220; SV Plate 22

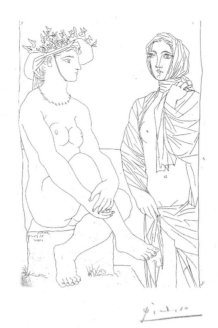

8.12

8.13

8.14

126

8.15

8.16

8.17

8.15 BLIND MINOTAUR GUIDED BY A LITTLE GIRL WITH BUNCH OF FLOWERS (illus. p. 71)
Minotaure aveugle guidé par une petite fille avec fleurs
September 22, 1934, Boisgeloup
Drypoint, scraper, and burin
25.1 x 34.7 cm
Baer 434 XII.B.c; Bloch 222; SV Plate 94

8.16 BLIND MINOTAUR GUIDED BY A LITTLE GIRL WITH PIGEON
Minotaure aveugle guidé par une petite fille au pigeon
November 4, 1934
Etching, burin, and scraper
22.6 x 31.3 cm
Baer 436 IV.B.c; Bloch 224; SV Plate 95

8.17 BLIND MINOTAUR GUIDED BY MARIE-THERESE WITH PIGEON ON A STARRY NIGHT (illus. p. 17)
Minotaure aveugle guidé par Marie-Thérèse au pigeon, dans une nuit étoilée
December 1934–January 1935, Paris
Aquatint, scraper, drypoint, and burin
24.0 x 34.0 cm
Baer 437 IV.B.c; Bloch 225; SV Plate 97

8.18

8.19

8.18 TAVERN SCENE WITH YOUNG CATALAN FISHERMAN TELLING HIS LIFE STORY TO AN OLD BEARDED FISHERMAN

La Taberna, jeune pêcheur Catalan racontant sa vie à un vieux pêcheur barbu
November 29, 1934, Paris
Etching
23.6 x 29.6 cm
Baer 442 B.c; Bloch 228; SV Plate 12

In this allegory of life's travels a young man (Picasso) talks with an old man (who resembles Rembrandt).

8.19 HARPY WITH BULL'S HEAD AND FOUR LITTLE GIRLS ON A TOWER TOPPED WITH BLACK FLAG

Harpye à tête de taureau, et quatre petites filles sur une tour surmontée d'un drapeau noir
December 1934, Paris
Etching
23.7 x 29.7 cm
Baer 444 B.c; Bloch 229; SV Plate 13

8.20 FAUN UNVEILING A SLEEPING WOMAN ("JUPITER AND ANTIOPE" AFTER REMBRANDT) (illus. p. 73)

Faune dévoilant une dormeuse ("Jupiter et Antiope" d'après Rembrandt)
June 12, 1936, Paris
Sugar-lift aquatint and scraper
31.3 x 41.3 cm
Baer 609 VI.B.c; Bloch 230; SV Plate 27

8.20

8.21 PORTRAIT OF AMBROISE VOLLARD. II
Portrait de Ambroise Vollard. II
March 4, 1937
Sugar-lift aquatint and scraper
34.5 x 24.3 cm
Baer 619 B.c; Bloch 231; SV Plate 98

The last three plates in the suite are portraits of Vollard.

8.21

9. WOMAN BULLFIGHTER, LAST KISS? (illus. p. 69)
Femme torero, dernier baiser?
June 12, 1934, Paris
Etching, printed by Lacourière
on vellum
51.3 x 29.4 cm
Signed and numbered in red ink: 2/3
Baer 425 B; Bloch 1329

This and the following scene (cat. 10) focus on the violence of the bullfight, a subject that was seen only in passing in the *Suite Vollard*. A charging bull, a gored horse, and a helpless woman (Marie-Thérèse) are intertwined in a dance of death; see Gilmour, "Marie-Thérèse: A Perfect Odalisque."

9

10. THE GREAT BULLFIGHT, WITH WOMAN BULLFIGHTER
La Grande Corrida, avec femme torero
September 8, 1934, Boisgeloup
Etching, printed by Lacourière on Montval wove paper
49.5 x 69.2 cm
Unsigned and unnumbered, from the 1939 edition
Baer 433 C; Bloch 1330

10

11. HISTOIRE NATURELLE

Natural History
by George Louis Leclerc, comte de Buffon, 1942, Paris
Published by Martin Fabiani
Book with 31 etchings and sugar-lift aquatints
Printed by Lacourière on Vidalon wove paper with *Vollard* watermark
Not signed, but numbered on the colophon: *150* (of 226)

The French literary classic provided only a point of departure for Picasso's brilliant use of sugar-lift aquatint, accomplished with the help of the printer Lacourière. The illustrations, commissioned by Vollard, were completed in 1936, but because of Vollard's death remained unpublished until 1942.

11.1

11.1 THE SPANISH BULL
El Toro espagnol
1936, Paris
Sugar-lift aquatint, scraper, drypoint, and burin
29.5 x 24.0 cm
Baer 578 III.B.ß.5;
Bloch 331; Plate 4

11.2 THE CRAYFISH
La Langouste
1936, Paris
Sugar-lift aquatint and drypoint
32.0 x 22.4 cm
Baer 599 III.B.ß.5;
Bloch 352; Plate 25

11.2

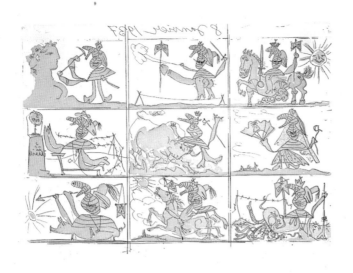

12.1

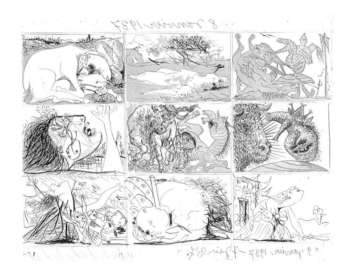

12.2

12. DREAMS AND LIES OF FRANCO

Sueño y Mentira de Franco
1937, Paris
Published by Picasso
Portfolio with 2 etchings and
aquatints with wrappers and text
Printed on Montval laid paper
Stamped signature.
Numbered: *28/850*

In an intense small format
(Picasso had intended them to
be cut up and used as
postcards) of nine scenes
Picasso protests against Franco's
fascist forces. The sequence of
the three rows of caricatures on
the first plate starts in the upper
right corner, with Franco setting
off on horseback. The first plate
was completed in January as
were five scenes on the second.
After the bombing of Guernica
on April 26, Picasso completed
the second plate in May, adding
four scenes of anguish and
death. His handwritten text of
outrage was included in the
published portfolio.

12.1 PLATE I
January 8, Paris
Etching and sugar-lift aquatint
31.2 x 41.7 cm
Baer 615 II.B.e; Bloch 297

12.2 PLATE II
January 8–9; June 7, Paris
Etching and sugar-lift aquatint
31.2 x 41.8 cm
Baer 616 V.B.e; Bloch 298

13. HEAD OF A WOMAN, NO. 3 (PORTRAIT OF DORA MAAR)

Tête de femme, no. 3
(Portrait de Dora Maar)
January–June 1939, Paris
Aquatint and scraper (plate 4 of 4
used in a complex color print)
Printed by Lacourière, proofs on
thin Japan paper
Each signed and annotated:
épreuve d'état
Baer 651; Bloch 1339

In 1939 Picasso spent several
months working with Lacourière
systematically exploring the
possibilities of color intaglio.
The two proofs exhibited here
are from a long series of color
experiments, based on a portrait
of his mistress Dora Maar (see
Baer 647, 648, 650, 651).

13.1

13.1 HEAD OF A WOMAN, NO. 3 (PORTRAIT OF DORA MAAR)

(Color Plate 1)
Proof, possibly before the plate was
steel-faced, printed in Prussian blue
from plate 4
30.9 x 24.0 cm
Baer 651 A. (4th plate) I; Bloch 1339

13.2 HEAD OF A WOMAN, NO. 3 (PORTRAIT OF DORA MAAR)

Proof printed in black from plate 4
32.6 x 24.6 cm
Baer 651 A. (4th plate) VII.a; Bloch 1339

13.2

2. LITHOGRAPHS AND OTHER PRINTS, 1945–1958

Of Picasso's more than four hundred lithographs, his most original work dates to the initial period at Fernand Mourlot's workshop. Many earlier and later prints represent a rapid sketch that was transferred to stone, making it essentially a reproduction of a drawing, not an engagement with the technique of lithography.

Lithography assumed primacy over other printmaking techniques for a relatively brief period in Picasso's career. Adams, in his essay "Picasso's Lithographs, 1945–1949," describes the burst of creativity that began in late 1945 and continued unabated into early 1946, making it it clear how Picasso moved from working on one stone to another, altering and developing several compositions simultaneously.

Among the lithographs in the Norton Simon Museum are an unusual number of proofs. Simon bought 228 lithographs in 1977 from the collection of Fernand Mourlot. Included in that purchase were many proofs reserved for the artist from the crucial period of 1945–46, when the separate editions generally numbered 18 impressions. Impressions reserved for the artist were printed on Arches wove paper, like those of the published edition, but they were not signed or numbered. Simon's purchase included 168 *bon à tirer* proofs, and seven dedicated to Mourlot. Simon continued to seek out impressions that were unique or special, including trial proofs.

PIGEON ON GRAY BACKGROUND (cat. 21, see p. 141)   21

14. TWO NUDE WOMEN

Deux femmes nues
November 10, 1945–February 12, 1946, Paris
Lithograph, with pen, wash, scraper, and crayon, on stone
Of the four states cited below, the first two proofs were
printed on various papers; the last two on Arches wove paper
Mourlot 16 i–xviii; Bloch 390

Adams traces the transformation of this composition. The
early states of Picasso's lithographs of the winter 1945–46
were printed only in groups of 18 proofs reserved for the
artist. Mourlot's catalogue cites 19 impressions for this print
(rather than what became the usual 18) of all 18 states as
well as an edition of 50 of the final state.

14.1 TWO NUDE WOMEN
December 30, 1945–January 5, 1946
33.0 x 40.4 cm
On the verso is a lithograph by
another artist.
Mourlot 16, unrecorded trial
proof between states vii and viii

14.1

14.2

14.3

14.4

14.2 TWO NUDE WOMEN
January 24, 1946
27.1 x 37.1 cm
On the verso is another impression
of the lithograph by the unknown
artist cited opposite.
Provenance: Marie-Thérèse Walter
Mourlot 16 xii/xviii, trial proof

14.3 TWO NUDE WOMEN
January 31, 1946
27.0 x 36.0 cm
Annotated first: *15e*, crossed out,
then: *14e*
Mourlot 16 xiv/xviii, trial proof

14.4 TWO NUDE WOMEN
February 1, 1946
27.0 x 36.2 cm
Mourlot 16 xv/xviii (1 of 19
artist-reserved proofs)

15. THE BULL

Le Taureau
December 5, 1945–January 17, 1946, Paris
Lithograph, worked first with wash, then
pen, scraper, and crayon, on stone
Mourlot 17 i–xi; Bloch 389

The Mourlot catalogue of Picasso's lithographs, while generally reliable in its
documentation, is at times incomplete; for example, it does not include all
states for this print—meaning that Picasso worked on the stones unobserved
and unknown to Mourlot. The Norton Simon Museum impression (cat. 15.2)
clearly shows the composition between states one and two, as described by
Mourlot. This undescribed trial proof between i and ii and the trial proof of
the xi and final state (on the verso is an impression of *Two Nude Women*) were
printed on various papers at hand in the workshop, in distinction to the 18
proofs reserved for the artist, printed on Arches wove paper.

15.1

15.1 THE BULL
December 5, 1945
32.4 x 43.4 cm
Mourlot 17 i/xi
(1 of 18 artist-reserved proofs)

15.2 THE BULL
December 12, 1945
32.1 x 48.6 cm
Mourlot 17 i–ii/xi, trial proof

15.3 THE BULL
December 24, 1945
31.5 x 44.0 cm
Mourlot 17 v/xi
(1 of 18 artist-reserved proofs)

15.4 THE BULL
December 26, 1945
31.0 x 44.2 cm
Mourlot 17 vi/xi
(1 of 18 artist-reserved proofs)

15.2

15.3

15.4

15.5 THE BULL
January 5, 1946
30.7 x 43.5 cm
Mourlot 17 ix/xi
(1 of 18 artist-reserved proofs)

15.6 THE BULL
January 17, 1946
29.0 x 40.5 cm
Inscribed: *Marie-Thérèse Walter*
Provenance: Marie-Thérèse Walter
Printed on the verso of *Two Nude Women*
Mourlot 17 xi/xi, trial proof

15.5

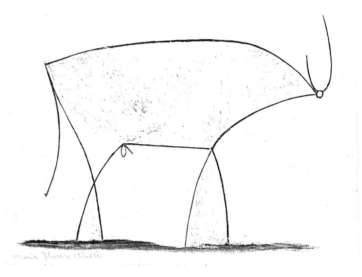

15.6

16. BULLS, RAMS, AND BIRDS
Taureaux, béliers et oiseaux
December 22, 1945, Paris
Lithograph, crayon drawing
transferred to stone
30.4 x 39.9 cm
Mourlot 21; Bloch 1344
(1 of 18 artist-reserved proofs)

16

17

17. BULLFIGHT UNDER A BLACK SUN
Corrida au soleil noir
January 7, 1946, Paris
Lithograph, ink and crayon
drawing transferred to stone
30.5 x 41.5 cm
Printed on Arches wove paper
Signed and annotated in red chalk:
Bon à tirer à 50 épreuves
Mourlot 25; Bloch 1346

The English edition of the Mourlot
catalogue does not cite an edition
of 50, only 18 proofs; Bloch does
not cite any edition.

18. SIDE VIEW OF BULL
Taureau de profil
December 25, 1945, Paris
Lithograph, crayon drawing
transferred to stone
29.6 x 42.3 cm
Mourlot 27 (1 of 18 artist-
reserved proofs); not in Bloch

18

19. EIGHT SILHOUETTES
Huit silhouettes
January 13, 1946, Paris
Lithograph, cut-out paper and
crayon drawing transferred to
stone
31.9 x 43.9 cm
Signed and annotated in red
crayon: *Bon à tirer*
Mourlot 29; Bloch 388

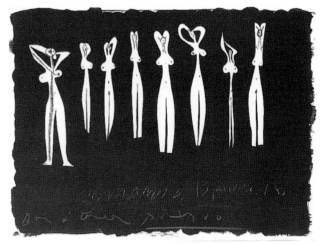

19

20. THE PIPERS

Les Pipeaux
August–September 1946, Golfe Juan
Etching, scraper, and drypoint on zinc
Printed by Louis Fort
Published by Galerie Louise Leiris
Baer 731 I–VI; Bloch 1347–49

In several closely related drawings (Zervos XIV,
nos. 225–29, 232) of August 26 and 28, as well
as in the six states of the print, Picasso explored
the relationship of three figures: two fauns, one
playing a flute, another who sometimes stands
on his head, and a central figure of a dancing
nymph/woman, who sometimes holds a tambourine.

20.1 THE PIPERS
27.0 x 35.5 cm
Proof printed on Arches wove paper
Inscribed and numbered in red crayon:
1er Etat 1/2
Baer 731 I/VI; Bloch 1347

20.1

20.2 THE PIPERS
(illus. p. 3)
27.1 x 35.2 cm
Proof printed on J. Perrigot
MBM wove paper
Inscribed and numbered:
3e Etat 1/1
Baer 731 III/VI; Bloch 1348

20.3 THE PIPERS
27.3 x 35.3 cm
Proof printed in green on
Japan paper
Annotated and numbered:
6e Etat 2/2
Baer 731 VI/VI; Bloch 1349

20.2

**21. PIGEON ON GRAY
BACKGROUND**
(illus. p. 133)
Pigeon au fond gris
February 2, 1947, Paris
Lithograph, gouache and wash
drawing transferred to stone
27.6 x 48.3 cm
Signed and annotated in green
crayon: *Bon à tirer*
Mourlot 64; Bloch 418

20.3

**22. COMPOSITION
WITH VASE OF
FLOWERS**
(Color Plate 2)
Composition au vase de fleurs
March 10, 1947, Paris
Lithograph, printed in three
colors: black from a zinc plate,
red cutouts from transfer to
stone, and gray on stone
45.5 x 60.2 cm
Printed on BFK Rives wove
paper
Signed and annotated in red
ink: *Bon à tirer*
Mourlot 74; Bloch 426

22

23. "DAVID AND BATHSHEBA" (AFTER LUCAS CRANACH)

"David et Bethsabée" (d'après Lucas Cranach)
March 30, 1947–April 17, 1949, Paris
Lithograph, with pen and wash, scraped and redrawn, on zinc
Mourlot 109 i–x; Bloch 439–41

The composition is after the painting is in the Dahlem Gemäldegalerie in Berlin which Picasso knew from a postcard (illus. p. 53).

At the end of March after working the zinc plate through five states, Picasso put it aside. A year later, in March 1948, he returned to it, reworked it, and transferred the composition to stone. Another year passed. Then in March and April 1949 he removed almost all work from the zinc plate and essentially redrew the composition.

23.1

23.1 "DAVID AND BATHSHEBA" (AFTER LUCAS CRANACH)
March 30, 1947
65.0 x 50.0 cm
Signed and annotated in orange crayon:
Bon à tirer pour 50 épreuves
Mourlot 109 i/x; Bloch 439

23.2 "DAVID AND BATHSHEBA" (AFTER LUCAS CRANACH)
March 30, 1947
65.0 x 47.6 cm
Signed and annotated in blue crayon:
Bon à tirer
Mourlot 109 ii/x; Bloch 440

23.2

**23.3 "DAVID AND BATHSHEBA"
(AFTER LUCAS CRANACH)**
March 30, 1947
65.0 x 48.7 cm
Signed and numbered: *5/50*
Mourlot 109 iv/x; Bloch 441

23.3

**24. "DAVID AND BATHSHEBA"
(AFTER LUCAS CRANACH)**
"David et Bethsabée" (d'après Cranach)
March 30, 1948–April 7, 1949, Paris
Lithograph, transferred from state vi
of preceding zinc to stone
65.1 x 47.5 cm
Signed and dedicated: *Pour Fernand Mourlot*
Mourlot 109A i/i; Bloch 442

The Norton Simon Museum also has an
impression from the edition of 50, which
is not cited either in the French or the
English edition of Mourlot, but is in Bloch.

24

25. COMPOSITION

November 21, 1948, Paris
Lithograph, drawn with crayon,
ink, and scraper on zinc
64.6 x 49.8 cm
Signed and annotated: *Bon à tirer*
Mourlot 127; Bloch 578

On November 20 Picasso made the first of a
group of portraits of Françoise Gilot (Mourlot
126) in which he began with the same flat
black background and then worked with
scraper, sandpaper, and needle. On the next
day he made five heads (Mourlot 127–31), of
which only this is not recognizable as a head.

26. WOMAN IN AN ARMCHAIR, NO. 4 (FROM THE VIOLET ZINC PLATE) (illus. p. 19)

Femme au fauteuil, No. 4 (d'après le violet)
December 10, 1948–January 3, 1949, Paris
Lithograph, in wash on zinc
69.6 x 54.7 cm
Signed and numbered: *38/50*
Mourlot 137 v/v; Bloch 588

Neither the French nor English translation of
the Mourlot catalogues cites an edition of 50,
but it is listed in Bloch.

In November 1948 Picasso made a color
lithograph of Françoise Gilot in an armchair,
using five zinc plates (Mourlot 133), with
which he was not satisfied. During the next
two months, he reworked the individual color
plates through variant compositions printed
only in black. In all, more than twenty-five
such variant states exist.

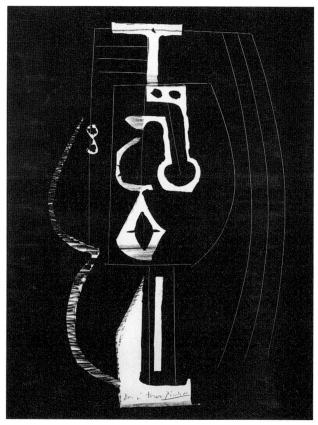

25

26

27

27. THE DOVE

La Colombe
January 9, 1949, Paris
Lithograph, in wash on zinc
54.8 x 69.7 cm
Signed and dedicated: *Bon à tirer pour Mourlot*
Mourlot 141; Bloch 583

Both Picasso and Matisse kept pigeons as pets. (As a child Picasso had helped his father who often made paintings of them, the son painting their feet.) Throughout his life Picasso kept many animals as pets—dogs, cats, owls, even a monkey, as well as exotic birds and pigeons and doves.

This lithograph is remarkable for the delicacy and subtlety of the gray washes. The composition became celebrated when it was reproduced as a poster of the dove of peace after the end of the Second World War.

28

28. THE LOBSTER

Le Hommard
January 9, 1949, Paris
Lithograph, in wash on zinc
54.8 x 69.8 cm
Signed and annotated: *Bon à tirer*
Mourlot 143; Bloch 584

29. THE TOAD

Le Crapaud
January 13, 1949, Paris
Lithograph, in wash on zinc
49.7 x 64.2 cm
Signed and annotated: *Bon à tirer*
Mourlot 144; Bloch 585

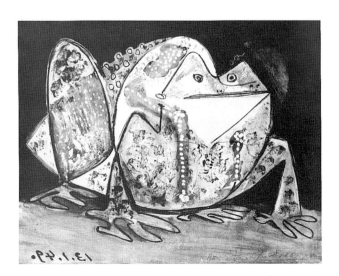

29

30

30. THE CHECKERED BLOUSE

Le Corsage à carreaux
March 26, 1949, Paris
Lithograph, from a transfer of the
black stone of Mourlot 175
64.9 x 49.6 cm
Signed and annotated: *Bon à tirer pour Mourlot*
Mourlot 175A; Bloch 601

31. FRANÇOISE AGAINST A GRAY BACKGROUND

Françoise sur fond gris
November 5, 1950, Paris
Lithograph, with crayon and
wash, on zinc
64.3 x 47.9 cm
Signed and annotated: *Bon à tirer*
Mourlot 195 ii/ii; Bloch 681

31

32. "THE ITALIAN WOMAN" (AFTER VICTOR ORSEL'S PICTURE)

"L'Italienne" (d'après le tableau de Victor Orsel)
January 18–21, 1953, Paris
Lithograph, with brush and engraving tool over screened photolithograph on zinc
44.7 x 37.8 cm
Not printed until 1955
Signed and annotated: *Bon à tirer*
Mourlot 238 ii/ii; Bloch 740

In the Mourlot workshop Picasso found a zinc plate with a commercial reproduction and improvised on it.

33. GAMES AND READING

Les Jeux et la lecture
January 23–24, 1953, Paris
Lithograph on zinc
48.0 x 63.0 cm
Signed and annotated: *Bon à tirer*
Mourlot 240; Bloch 741

This scene of Gilot with her two small children was not editioned until 1958. Mourlot cites only 5 artist-reserved proofs, but Bloch cites an edition of 50.

32

33

34. DANCE OF THE BANDERILLAS

La Danse des banderilles
February 14, 1954, Vallauris
Lithograph, transferred from
a crayon drawing, to stone
47.5 x 64.0 cm
Signed and annotated: *Bon à tirer*
Mourlot 248; Bloch 752

35. "WOMEN OF ALGIERS" (AFTER DELACROIX). I

"Femmes d'Alger" (d'après Delacroix). I
January 20, 1955, Paris
Lithograph, with an engraving
needle on a blackened stone
27.9 x 35.0 cm
Mourlot 265 (1 of 5 artist-reserved
proofs); not in Bloch

In late 1954 and early 1955 Picasso,
while at work on an extended series
of oils after Delacroix, made two
lithographs using the same complex
technique of the Cranach lithographs
(cats. 23 and 24). Jacqueline Roque
is the model for the odalisque seated
at the left.

36. "WOMEN OF ALGIERS" (AFTER DELACROIX). II

"Femmes d'Alger" (d'après Delacroix). II
February 5–March 17, 1955, Paris
Lithograph, with engraving needle, crayon, and scrumbles on stone
Mourlot 266 i–iv; not in Bloch

36.1 "WOMEN OF ALGIERS" (AFTER DELACROIX). II
March 7, 1955
23.3 x 33.7 cm
Mourlot 266 ii/iv
(1 of 5 artist-reserved proofs)

36.2 "WOMEN OF ALGIERS" (AFTER DELACROIX). II
March 17, 1955
23.4 x 33.7 cm
Mourlot 266 iv/iv
(1 of 5 artist-reserved proofs)

36.1

36.2

37. WOMAN WITH HAIRNET
(Color Plate 3)
La Femme à résille
September 1956
Lithograph, transfer from drawings for 4 zinc plates in green, violet, bistre, and black
66.3 x 50.0 cm
Signed and annotated: *Bon à tirer*
Mourlot 178A iv/iv; Bloch 612

This portrait of Gilot is a later reworking of *Woman with Green Hair (Femme aux cheveux verts)* of March and April 1949 (Mourlot 178 and 178 A).

37

38. LA TAUROMAQUIA

The Art of the Bullfight
by José Delgado, alias Pepe Illo
1959, Barcelona
Book with 26 sugar-lift aquatints
Published by Gustavo Gili
Printed by Lacourière-Frélaut on
wove Guarro paper with watermark
of a bull's head
Signed and numbered on the
colophon: *XVI*
From the deluxe edition of 30 with
a second suite of prints

Picasso illustrated the same text as
Goya had in his 1816 suite of 33
etchings. Goya showed the early
history of the bullfight with Moors
fighting bulls in open fields, followed
by portrayals of illustrious matadors,
including Pepe Illo and his death in
the ring, as well as a scene where a
bull escapes into the grandstand.
Picasso's choice and handling of
scenes is, in contrast, lighthearted,
from the first scene of bulls calmly
grazing in a meadow, to the
procession into the ring, and various
phases of the bullfight. Even the
final end is treated with brio.

**38.1 PRICKING THE BULL WITH
A PAIR OF BANDERILLAS**
Clavando un par de banderillas
May 1957, Cannes
20.0 x 29.7 cm
Baer 984 B.d; Bloch 964; Plate 14

38.2 LANCING THE BULL
Alanceando a un toro
May 1957, Cannes
19.9 x 29.5 cm
Baer 996 B.d; Bloch 976; Plate 26

38.1

38.2

39

39. PORTRAIT OF DANIEL-HENRY KAHNWEILER. II

June 3, 1957, Cannes
Lithograph, transferred from
a crayon drawing to zinc
65.2 x 50.1 cm
Signed and annotated in blue crayon:
Bon à tirer
Mourlot 296; Bloch 835

One of three sketches of his dealer Picasso
drew on the same day (Mourlot 295-97).

40. BUST IN PROFILE

Buste de profile
December 27, 1958, Cannes
Lithograph on zinc
64.0 x 49.7 cm
Signed and annotated in red crayon:
Bon à tirer
Mourlot 306 iii/iii; Bloch 845

Picasso began this profile portrait of
Françoise Gilot in December 1957 and
an edition was printed; however, he
reworked it the following January and
again that December. Although this
impression is annotated *Bon à tirer*,
according to Mourlot there was no
edition printed of the third state.

41. WOMAN WITH FLOWERED BLOUSE

(illus. p. 6)
Femme au corsage à fleurs
December 27, 1958, Cannes
Lithograph, worked with wash and
engraving needle, on zinc
63.0 x 48.0 cm
Signed and annotated in red crayon:
Bon à tirer
Mourlot 307 iii/iii; Bloch 847

Again Picasso first drew this portrait
of Gilot in December 1957, reworked
it in February 1958, and finally
completed it the following December.

40

41

3. LINOCUTS, 1959–1962

Only two isolated linocuts predate 1953–54, when Picasso cut several designs to serve as posters for exhibitions at Vallauris. With the printer Hidalgo Arnéra and his workshop nearby, Picasso began to explore the technique of printing with four or more colors. The large linocut after Cranach of 1958 (cat. 42) was printed from five blocks, each inked a different color, in the traditional chiaroscuro woodcut technique.

Within a year, however, Picasso, tired of this tedious and piecemeal approach and devised an unorthodox and radical solution of using only a single block, which he worked with a gouge, a penknife, and various scrapers. After printing the preliminary design in one color, he recut and refined the composition, and printed the block in a second color, and later in a third. Then to improve the clarity of the colors, Picasso printed a cream tone over the entire sheet of paper and printed the additional colors on this surface. He also experimented (as had Edvard Munch) with cutting the block into segments and inking them separately. In all, Picasso's infatuation with the linocut lasted less than five years, but in his prodigal way he created some hundred prints.

Picasso's palette for many of the linocuts is limited to a range of earth tones—soft tans and browns. The sequence in which the colors were printed progressed from light to dark, from cream to caramel, to light brown, and was completed by the dominant black design printed over the accumulated muted tones. This restricted palette reflects to some degree his own work at the time in ceramics, as well as his knowledge of Greek black-figured Attic vases. At the other extreme to the earth tones is the high color of such works as the print after Lucas Cranach (cat. 42) and a still life (cat. 52). In both, strong yellows and reds vie for attention, as do the dense decorative patternings of lines.

In subject, the linocuts of 1959 begin with a series of bullfight scenes, a subject Picasso had recently explored with brevity and wit in a series of aquatints (cat. 38). The small, highly animated aquatints show the setting of the arena and the massed crowd, but in the linocuts, Picasso focused on the interaction and drama of the main participants, who are presented at close range. The embroidered costume of the matador is made much of and delight is taken in the swirling cape; the bull seems to dance rather than charge (cats. 43–45).

Among the most high-spirited linocuts are several bacchanals, one in which a goat cavorts with dancers and a musician under an azure sky (cat. 47, see also cover), another with an owl watching over the revels (cat. 48).

Certain subjects appear both as lithographs and as linocuts, as do several heads of women (cat. 46). The linocuts are far bolder and more summarily treated, as appropriate to the technique. Some linocuts offer fanciful take-offs of old masters; others serve as a vehicle for involuted linear and sculptural patterns of women's hats (cat. 51). Among the most arresting images is *Head of a Faun*, in which Picasso superimposed a masklike outline, cut with a heavy gouge, on a realistic head which was scratched and scraped with something like steel wool (cat. 50).

The appeal of Picasso's linocuts lies in their decorative and spirited character, the bold patterns and unconventional use of the medium. All the linocuts were published by the Galerie Louise Leiris either in 1960 (cats. 42–48) or in 1963 (cats. 49–52). Norton Simon's first large purchase of Picasso prints was the one hundred linocuts he acquired in 1964.

42. "PORTRAIT OF A YOUNG WOMAN" (AFTER LUCAS CRANACH THE YOUNGER). II (Color Plate 4)

"Portrait de jeune fille" (d'après Cranach le Jeune). II
July 4, 1958, Cannes
Linocut, printed from five blocks in bister, yellow, red, blue, and black
65.0 x 53.2 cm
Signed and numbered: *3/50*
Baer 1053 III.C.a; Bloch 859

44. PICADOR AND BULL

(Color Plate 7)
Picador et taureau
August 30, 1959, Cannes
Linocut, printed three times from a single block, first in beige, then in brown, and last in black
53.2 x 64.2 cm
Signed and numbered: *14/50*
Baer 1226 II.B.a; Bloch 909

45. PICADOR AND BULL

(Color Plate 6)
Picador et taureau
September 5–6, 1959, Cannes
Linocut, printed four times from a single block, first in beige, then in chocolate, brown, and last in black
53.2 x 64.1 cm
Signed and numbered: *14/50*
Baer 1229 IV.B.a; Bloch 907

43. THE BANDERILLERO

August 26, 1959, Cannes
Linocut, printed three times from a single block, first in beige, then in brown, and last in black
53.5 x 66.2 cm
Signed and numbered: *14/50*
Baer 1225 IV.B.a; Bloch 940

46. PORTRAIT OF JACQUELINE LEANING ON HER ELBOWS (Color Plate 12)

Portrait de Jacqueline accoudée
October 2, 1959, Cannes
Linocut, printed from a single block, first in black and then in cream
64.3 x 53.3 cm
Signed and numbered: *14/50*
Baer 1240 B.a; Bloch 922

47. BACCHANAL WITH YOUNG GOAT AND ONLOOKER
(illus. on cover; also Color Plate 8)
Bacchanale avec chevreau et spectateur
November 27, 1959, Cannes
Linocut, printed six times from three blocks in five colors, first in beige, then in green, blue, white, and last in black
52.7 x 63.7 cm
Signed and numbered: *14/50*
Baer 1260 III.B.f.2α; Bloch 931

49. VARIATION ON MANET'S "DEJEUNER SUR L'HERBE" (illus. p. 22)
Variation sur "Le Déjeuner sur l'herbe" de Manet
July 4 and November 23–24, 1961, Mougins
Linocut printed in black
53.2 x 64.1 cm
Signed and numbered: *29/50*
Baer 1277 I.B.a; Bloch 1023

51. LARGE HEAD OF A WOMAN IN A HAT
(Color Plate 10)
Grande tête de femme au chapeau
February 9, 1962, Mougins
Linocut printed four times from one block, first in beige, then in chestnut, chocolate, and last in black
64.1 x 52.8 cm
Signed and numbered: *44/50*
Baer 1293 IV.B.a; Bloch 1078

48. BACCHANAL WITH OWL
(Color Plate 9)
Bacchanale au hibou
December 2, 1959, Cannes
Linocut printed from one block in black and caramel
53.2 x 64.2 cm
Signed and numbered: *14/50*
Baer 1265 B.a; Bloch 938

50. HEAD OF A FAUN
(Color Plate 11)
Tête de faune
February 7, 1962, Mougins
Linocut printed from two blocks, first in brown, then in black
64.2 x 52.6 cm
Signed and numbered: *44/50*
Baer 1291 VI.B.b.2α; Bloch 1094

52. STILL LIFE WITH GLASS UNDER THE LAMP
(Color Plate 5)
Nature morte au verre sous la lampe
March 19, 1962, Mougins
Linocut printed from one block in four colors, yellow, red, green, and black
52.8 x 63.9 cm
Signed and numbered: *15/50*
Baer 1312 V.B.a; Bloch 1101

4. SUITE 347, 1968

When at eighty-seven Picasso returned to printmaking, he was in a very different mood from that in which he created the exuberant linocuts. *Suite 347* shows him in an introspective, at times confessional, frame of mind. Oppressed by his celebrity, the privacy of printmaking became an additional attraction. Between March and early October 1968 he created more than 300 etchings and aquatints (some days completing two or three plates), in collaboration with the printers Aldo and Piero Crommelynck at Mougins. The Galerie Louise Leiris late in 1968 began to exhibit some prints from *Suite 347*, completing the editioning in 1969. Picasso held one further engagement with printmaking in 1970, completing 156 plates.

Even at his advanced age, Picasso, aided by the Crommelynck brothers, was able to work in technically innovative ways, which greatly facilitated his output. Baer has described how the artist painted with liquid varnish directly on the plate; how he also bit directly into resin-grained plates. And in another technique, how Picasso created a negative effect, similar to that of a mezzotint, by drawing with a crayon made of varnish, which created white tonal highlights against a blackened background.

Baer's detailed catalogue notes help identify scenes that refer obliquely to contemporary subjects from radio or TV, political events, student riots, the assassination of Robert Kennedy, caricatures of French leaders, or a song by Edith Piaf. Barr-Sharrar has discussed the autobiographical character of this series (see Bibliography).

Literature again provided stimuli. Balzac's *Chef-d'oeuvre inconnu* appears briefly (cat. 53.10). Of more sustained interest was Fernando de Rojas's Spanish play *Celestina: The Tragi-Comedy of Calixtus and Melibe,* a picaresque tale of the old procuress Celestina, an inveterate liar who tricks many, particularly the young lovers Calixtus and Melibe. Mixing dark humor with hilarity, Picasso sketched moonlit flights with cloak-and-dagger chases and visits to her brothel (cats. 53.13 and 53.15).

Other recurring subjects include performances, some featuring the artist in a major role (cat. 53.3) or as a spectator reviewing the drama of his life and his life work (cats. 53.1 and 53.18). In contrast to the circus performers of the Blue Period drypoints, the performers of 1968 are a boisterous lot and include family, friends, and mistresses who vie for attention.

The traditions of European painting were never far from Picasso's mind. El Greco's *Burial of Count Orgaz* is recalled and parodied in an etching in which Picasso introduced family portraits, in particular of his artist father (cat. 53.22). Homage is paid to Goya in a scene of women in prison (cat. 53.23). Rembrandt, whose calligraphic caricature was seen in the *Suite Vollard* makes renewed appearances (cats. 53.11 and 53.16). Parodies of works by Titian, Poussin, Füssli (cat. 53.9), and others recur, but it is Ingres's painting *Raphael and La Fornarina* (Fine Arts Museums, Harvard University) that most deeply embedded itself in Picasso's psyche (cat. 53.25). Where Ingres's depiction of the famous artist seated with his beautiful model in his studio is a chaste image, Picasso imagines an explicit sexual encounter and adds the wicked touch of the pope as a Peeping Tom. Between August 29 and September 9, Picasso returned to this subject daily, some days creating two variants, in all twenty-four prints. In early October he returned to Balzac, Celestina, and Manet and later to the printer Piero Crommelynck and his family, whom he portrayed in his studio (Baer 1845–47), a fitting acknowledgment to the close collaboration of artist and printer that made the series possible. Simon acquired 110 prints from this extraordinary series in 1969 and 1970.

53. SUITE 347

March–August 1968, Mougins
Etchings, drypoints, and aquatints
Printed by Aldo and Piero Crommelynck
from steel-faced plates on Rives wove paper
Published by Galerie Louise Leiris, 1969
Each signed and numbered: *44/50*

Within a month of the death of Jaime Sabartés on February 13, 1968, Picasso began this series, dedicating proofs in his memory, which he later gave to the Picasso Museum in Barcelona. When published, the prints—as usual—had no titles because Picasso had no use for them. Baer's catalogue gives descriptive titles and adds Roman numerals following the date to indicate that several prints were made on the same day.

53.1

53.2

53.1 PICASSO, HIS WORK, AND HIS PUBLIC (illus. p. 25)
Picasso, son oeuvre, et son public
March 16–22
Etching
39.2 x 56.4 cm
Baer 1496 VII.B.b.1; Bloch 1481; Leiris 1

Picasso worked on the first plate of the series for seven days, taking it through as many states. A magician stands at the left, next to a small Picasso, who seems to hold the central scene in his hand in early states, but as work continued the right hand became a strange artificial (or skeletal) limb, which is almost obscured in the final state. The face has aged, with wrinkles under the chin. A spectator lounges below; at the right is a figure of a circus strongman; and in the center of the ring are a horse and female rider, seen against a sea of spectators' eyes.

53.2 SELF-PORTRAIT WITH A CANE, WITH ACTOR IN COSTUME, SATED LOVE, AND WOMEN
Autoportrait à la canne, avec comédien en costume, amour replet et femmes
March 25
Etching
42.1 x 34.5 cm
Baer 1503 B.b.1; Bloch 1488; Leiris 8

Picasso has depicted himself at the left, so short in stature that he resembles a dwarf, who only looks at but does not participate in the brothel scene.

53.3

53.4

53.5

53.3 DOUBLE SELF-PORTRAIT TRANSPOSED AND DREAMING OF THE CIRCUS WITH JACQUELINE AS AN ACROBAT, STANDING ON A BALL
(illus. p. 74)
Autoportrait transposé et dédoublé rêvant au cirque, avec Jacqueline en acrobate à la boule
March 26
Etching
31.4 x 41.6 cm
Baer 1504 B.b.1; Bloch 1489; Leiris 9

53.4 AT THE CIRCUS: ACROBATS, GIRAFFE, SWIMMERS. . .
(illus. p. 83)
Au cirque: Acrobates, girafe, nageuses . . .
April 11, I
Etching
31.4 x 46.1 cm
Baer 1520 B.b.1; Bloch 1504; Leiris 24

53.5 TELEVISION: ROMAN CHARIOT RACE. I
Télévision: Course de chars à l'antique. I
April 13, II
Aquatint, etching, with hand biting
31.6 x 39.2 cm
Baer 1530 B.b.1; Bloch 1514; Leiris 34

**53.6 EL GRECO AND REMBRANDT
SURROUNDED BY PORTRAITS**
(illus. p. 79)
Autour d'El Greco et Rembrandt:
Portraits
April 15 II, 17–19
Aquatint, scraper, and drypoint
22.3 x 31.9 cm
Baer 1536 II.B.b.1; Bloch 1520; Leiris 40

**53.7 AT THE CIRCUS: BAREBACK
RIDER, CLOWN, AND PIERROT**
Au cirque: Ecuyère, clown, et pierrot
April 19
Aquatint
31.6 x 39.2 cm
Baer 1538 B.b.1; Bloch 1522; Leiris 42

**53.8 PAINTER WITH COUPLE
AND CHILD**
Peintre avec couple et enfant
April 21, II
Etching
28.0 x 38.9 cm
Baer 1542 B.b.1; Bloch 1526; Leiris 46

The painter is one of many Rembrandtesque
references, seen in 17th-century dress as a
man with curly hair and beady eyes. Picasso
sees himself as wrinkled and old, with a
young woman and child.

53.6

53.7

53.8

53.9

53.9 FANTASY OF THE GENRE OF FÜSSLI'S "NIGHTMARE," WITH A VOYEUR UNDER THE BED

(illus. p. 89)
Fantaisie dans le genre du "Rêve de Füssli," avec voyeur sous le lit
April 28, II
Etching and drypoint
28.0 x 39.0 cm
Baer 1552 B.b.1; Bloch 1536; Leiris 56

Picasso is the voyeur crouched under the bed.

53.10 AROUND THE "UNKNOWN MASTERPIECE": THE PAINTER, MODEL, AND A COUPLE OF PAINTERS

Autour du "Chef-d'oeuvre inconnu": Peintre, modèle, couple et deux peintres
May 5, 6, 7, 9
Etching, scraper, and drypoint
41.2 x 49.5 cm
Baer 1560 V.B.b.1; Bloch 1544; Leiris 64

A return to Balzac's story (cat. 5) in which the old artist, Frenhofer, shows his masterpiece to his 17th-century contemporaries Poussin and Pourbus, who do not see or understand it.

53.11 REMBRANDTESQUE VISITOR AND PLAYFUL COURTESAN

Visiteur Rembranesque chez une courtisane folâtre
May 11, I
Etching
31.4 x 41.5 cm
Baer 1570 B.b.1; Bloch 1554; Leiris 74

53.10

53.11

**53.12 PICASSO THE TOURIST
RETURNS TO THE FOUNTAIN
OF CANALETAS**
(illus. p. 83)
*Retour aux sources: Picasso touriste
à la fuente de Canaletas*
May 13
Etching
41.2 x 49.4 cm
Baer 1577 B.b.1; Bloch 1561; Leiris 81

Baer notes that the fountain of Canaletas
in the Ramblas park in Barcelona is
famous and much reproduced on
postcards. The saying goes that if one
drinks its waters, one will return. Picasso
shows himself as a pilgrim arriving with
his artistic baggage and Spanish
entourage.

53.12

**53.13 SCENE FROM "THE
CELESTINA": THE GENTLEMAN
IS LED TO THE DIVE**
*Mise en scène de "La Célestine":
Le gentilhomme est entraîné
vers le bouge*
May 14, III
Etching, rebitten and reworked
29.5 x 34.8 cm
Baer 1581 B.b.1; Bloch 1565; Leiris 85

**53.14 THEATER OR TELEVISION:
CAPE AND SWORD**
Théâtre ou télévision: Cape et épée
May 15, II
Aquatint, scraper, and drypoint
29.5 x 34.7 cm
Baer 1583 III.B.b.1; Bloch 1567; Leiris 87

53.13

53.14

53.15

53.16

53.17

53.15 "THE CELESTINA": MOONLIT FLIGHT
"La Célestine": Fuite sous la lune
May 18, I
Aquatint, regrained and rebitten
29.5 x 34.7 cm
Baer 1595 B.b.1; Bloch 1579; Leiris 99

53.16 THEATER: AROUND REMBRANDT
(illus. p. 87)
Théâtre: Autour de Rembrandt
May 25, I
Aquatint, 1st state and sugar-lift
29.5 x 34.7 cm
Baer 1605 B.b.1; Bloch 1589; Leiris 109

Baer notes the abundance of references that can be read into this scene: Rembrandt's painting *Hendrickje on a Bed,* the figure of Rembrandt, the child (Picasso's son Paolo or the son of El Greco who appears in the *Burial of the Count of Orgaz*).

53.17 SPANISH NOTABLES VISITING A BROTHEL ORNAMENTED WITH A SUIT OF ARMOR
Notables espagnols visitant une maison close ornée d'une armure
May 26, IV
Etching
41.3 x 49.5 cm
Baer 1611 B.b.1; Bloch 1595; Leiris 115

This is the fourth print made on that day; two earlier ones refer to *The Celestina*.

53.18 OLD MAN THINKING OVER HIS LIFE: GALLANT YOUTH, MATURITY AS A FAMOUS PAINTER, WORK CREATED IN THE SLUMS NOW ENTHRONED BENEATH A CANOPY

(illus. p. 95)

Vieil homme songeant à sa vie: Jeunesse galante, âge mûr de peintre célèbre, œuvre créé dans un taudis et tronant maintenant sous un dais

May 28

Sugar-lift aquatint

49.3 x 33.5 cm

Baer 1619 B.b.1; Bloch 1604; Leiris 123

53.19 LADIES-IN-WAITING AND GENTLEMEN IN THE SIERRA

Ménines et gentilshommes dans la Sierra

June 1, I

Sugar-lift aquatint

33.6 x 49.4 cm

Baer 1630 B.b.1; Bloch 1614; Leiris 134

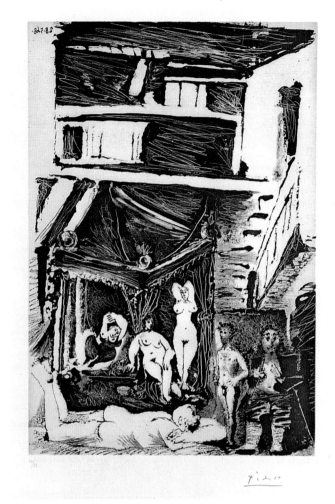

53.18

53.19

162

53.20

53.20 MEMORIES: CIRCUS WITH "THE GIANT" AND SELF-PORTRAIT AS BABY-OLD MAN

(illus. p. 91)
Souvenirs: Cirque, avec "El Gigante," et autoportrait en bébé-vieillard
June 4, II
Aquatint, etching, and scraper
used as drypoint
49.3 x 33.6 cm
Baer 1638 IV.B.b.1; Bloch 1622;
Leiris 142

53.21 VARIATION ON DON QUIXOTE AND DULCINEA: THE STROLLING PLAYERS MAKE A STOP

Variation autour de Don Quichotte et Dulcinée: Halte de comédiens ambulants
June 15, III
Sugar-lift aquatint
33.6 x 49.4 cm
Baer 1657 B.b.1; Bloch 1641;
Leiris 161

53.21

53.22 "THE BURIAL OF THE COUNT OF ORGAZ" (AFTER PICASSO)

"L'Enterrement du Comte d'Orgaz" (d'après Picasso)
June 30, I
Aquatint, etching, and scaper
28.0 x 38.9 cm
Baer 1692 III.B.b.1; Bloch 1676;
Leiris 196

53.23 REMEMBERING GOYA: WOMEN IN PRISON

En pensant à Goya: Femmes en prison
July 16, I
Sugar-lift aquatint
31.6 x 39.5 cm
Baer 1702 B.b.1; Bloch 1686;
Leiris 206

53.22

53.23

53.24 ABDUCTION. III
Enlèvement. III
July 28, I
Aquatint worked with
sandpaper (or pumice)
31.6 x 31.4 cm
Baer 1719 II.B.b.1;
Bloch 1703; Leiris 223

**53.25 RAPHAEL AND LA
FORNARINA, IV: WITH
THE POPE PULLING ASIDE
THE CURTAIN**
*Raphael et la Fornarina IV:
avec le pape tirant le rideau*
August 31, II
Etching
41.4 x 49.5 cm
Baer 1796 B.b.1;
Bloch 1779; Leiris 299

53.24

53.25

APPENDIX

**Checklist of the Norton Simon
Museum Collections of
Prints by Picasso
compiled by Sharon Goodman**

The following is a complete
checklist of the Picasso prints in
the Norton Simon Museum,
Foundation collections, and the
Simon personal collection. The
abbreviated information follows
the cataloguing employed
throughout this book, as cited in
"Notes on Catalogue Entries,"
p. 114.

Exceptions to these notes are:

References Baer 1986–96
numbers have been followed
for chronological order, except
where to do so interrupts the
sequence of a suite, such as *Suite
Vollard*. Prints preceded by an *
indicate a break in numerical
sequence.

Titles and dates Titles are
given in English and are often
abbreviated; only the year is
cited.

States Proofs or *bon à tirer* (BAT)
impressions are so identified.
Arabic numbers in parentheses
after the title indicates the
number of impressions. States are
cited after the description of the
medium. Artist's Reserved Proofs
are abbreviated ARP. Lithographic
states are cited in lower case
Roman numerals. Arabic numbers
in parentheses following indicate
the number of impressions of
that state.

Technique Lithographs are
cited without further technical
information.

Measurements These can be
found in the Baer, Bloch, or
Mourlot catalogues.

The checklist is divided into four
sections by catalogue:
1. Intaglio prints, 1905–59,
according to Baer.
2. Linocuts, according to Baer.
3. *Suite 347* intaglio prints,
1968, according to Baer.
4. Lithographs, according to
Mourlot.

1. INTAGLIO PRINTS

Circus Performers 1905
(illus. cat. 1.1)
Drypoint
Baer 9 II.b.2; Bloch 7

Salomé (2) 1905
Drypoint; proof before steel-
facing (1)
Edition: 250 (1) (illus. cat 1.2)
Baer 17 III.a and III.b.2; Bloch 14

SAINT MATOREL
(illus. cats. 2.1–2.2)
By Max Jacob
Published by Daniel-Henry
Kahnweiler, Paris, 1911
Book with 4 etchings printed
by Eugène Delâtre
Edition: 100, no. 23 / 85 on
Van Gelder laid paper, without
watermark
Signed and numbered on
colophon
Baer 23 II.b.3, Baer 24 b.3,
Baer 25 IV.b.3, Baer 26 b.3;
Bloch 19–22

Head of a Man with Pipe 1912
(illus. cat. 3)
Etching
Proof impression, signed
Baer 32 b; Bloch 23

Still Life with Bottle of Marc
1911
(illus. cat. 4)
Drypoint
Edition: 100, no. 23, signed
Baer 33 b; Bloch 24

The Three Friends 1927
Etching
Edition: 150, no. 124, signed
and numbered
Baer 117 II.b.2; Bloch 76

**THE UNKNOWN
MASTERPIECE** [*LE CHEF-
D'ŒUVRE INCONNU*]
(illus. cats. 5.1–5.3)
By Honoré de Balzac
Published by Ambroise Vollard,
Paris, 1931
Book with 13 etchings, printed
by Louis Fort; 63 wood
engravings; 16 reproductions
of Picasso's drawings
Edition: 340, no. XIV / XXX
(h.c.) on Rives wove paper,
some with BFK watermark
Signed and numbered on the
colophon
Baer 123 b.1.y–128 b.1.y, 129 II
b.1.y, 130 b.1.y–134 b.1.y, 135
II.b.1.y; Bloch 82–94
One impression from a separate
Edition: 63/99;
signed and numbered
Baer 130 b.2.α; Bloch 89

Nude Crowned with Flowers
Etching, BAT
Baer 142 B.a; Bloch 97

THE METAMORPHOSES
[*LES MÉTAMORPHOSES*]
(illus. cats. 6.1–6.3)
By Ovid
Published by Albert Skira,
Lausanne, 1931
Book with 30 etchings, printed
by Louis Fort
Edition: 145, no. XIV / XX (h.c.)
on Arches hand-made laid paper,
with *Arches à la main* watermark
Numbered on colophon
Baer 143 b.2.ß–147 b.2.ß, 148 II.
b.2.ß, 149 b.2.ß–153 b.2.ß, 154
II. b.2.ß, 155 b.2.ß–159 b.2.ß,
160 II.b.2.ß, 161 b.2.ß, 162
III.b.2.ß, 163 b.2.ß–172 b.2.ß;
Bloch 99–128

***Two Nude Women. II** 1930
Etching, BAT
Baer 199 b.1; Bloch 132

***The Diver (Marie-Thérèse)** (2)
1932 (illus. cat. 7)
Etching with collage
Edition: 100, signed
Baer 277 B.b; Bloch 1322

***Woman Bullfighter. Last
Kiss?** (2) 1934 (illus. cat. 9)
Etching on vellum, Edition 3,
no. 2. Signed and numbered;
Edition: 1 of 5 proofs
Baer 425 B and C; Bloch 1329

***The Great Bullfight, with
Woman Bullfighter** 1934
(illus. cat. 10)
Etching, edition: 50
Baer 433 C; Bloch 1330

SUITE VOLLARD
(illus. cats. 8.1–8.21)
Published by Ambroise Vollard,
Paris, 1939
100 etchings, aquatints, and drypoints, printed by Roger Lacourière
Edition: 50 on Montval laid
paper, with Montgolfier watermark
Signed in pencil, lower right,
on each sheet
Baer 192 B.c, 195 B.c, 201 B.c,
202 B.c, 203 II.B.c, 205 B.c, 207
B.c–210 B.c, 258 B.c, 296 II.B.c,
297 VI.B.c, 298 B.c, 299 VII.B.c,
300 B.c–303 B.c, 304 II.B.c, 305
B.c, 307 B.c, 308 II.B.c, 309
B.c–317 B.c, 319 B.c–326 B.c, 328
B.c, 330 B.c–332 B.c, 338 B.c,
340 II.B.c, 341 B.c, 342 XIV.B.c,
343 B.c–347 B.c, 348 III.B.c, 349
B.c, 350 B.c, 352 III.B.c, 353 B.c,
354 B.c, 355 II.B.c, 356 III.B.c,
363 B.c, 365 B.c–367 B.c, 369
II.B.c, 378 IX.B.c, 380 B.c, 384
IV.B.c, 385 VI.B.c, 404 B.c, 405
B.c, 406 III.B.c, 407 B.c, 408 B.c,
410 B.c, 411 B.c, 413 B.c, 414
B.c, 416 VI.B.c, 423 B.c, 424
V.B.c, 434 XII.B.c, 435 B.c, 436
IV.B.c, 437 IV.B.c, 440 III.B.c, 441
B.c, 442 B.c, 444 B.c, 609 VI.B.c,
617 B.c–619 B.c; Bloch 134-233
Nine impressions from a smaller
Edition: 9/15; signed and numbered
Baer 318 B.c, 327 B.c, 329 B.c,
351 III.B.c, 368 IV.B.c, 412 B.c,
421 B.c, 426 B.c, 427 B.c; Bloch
165, 174, 176, 192, 200, 213,
217, 220 221

NATURAL HISTORY
[*HISTOIRE NATURELLE*] 1936
(illus. cats. 11.1–11.2)
By Georges Louis Leclerc, comte
de Buffon
Published by Martin Fabiani,
Paris, 1942
Book with 31 etchings and
aquatints, some with burin and
drypoint, printed by Roger
Lacourière
Edition: 226, no.150 on wove
Vidalon paper with Ambroise or
Vollard watermark
Baer 575 II.B.ß.5, 576 IV.B.b.ß.5,
577 II.B.b.ß.5, 578 III.B.b.ß.5,
579 II.B.b.ß.5–583 II.B.b.ß.5, 584
B.ß.5, 585 B.ß.5, 586 II.B.ß.5,
587 B.ß.5–589 B.ß.5, 590
II.B.b.ß.5, 591 II.B.ß.5, 592
III.B.ß.5, 593 IV.B.ß.5, 594 B.ß.5,
595 III.B.ß.5, 596 II.B.ß.5, 597
II.B.ß.5, 598 III.B.b.ß.5, 599
III.B.b.ß.5, 600 II.B.ß.5–604
II.B.ß.5, 605 IV.B.b.ß.5; Bloch
328–358

**DREAMS AND LIES OF
FRANCO** [*SUEÑO Y MENTIRA
DE FRANCO*]
(illus. cats. 12.1–12.2)
Published by Picasso, Paris, 1937
2 etchings and aquatints with
wrappers and text, printed by
Roger Lacourière
Edition: 850, no. 28 on Montval
laid paper
Stamped signature; numbered
Baer 615 II.B.e, 616 V.B.e;
Bloch 297, 298

Man Making an Arc in . . .
1939
Drypoint; BAT
Baer 633 A.b; Bloch 305

**Head of Woman, No. 3
(Dora Maar)** (2) 1939
(illus. cats. 13.1–13.2)
Aquatint and scraper; one
unique proof
Baer 651 A.I and A.V11.a;
Bloch 1339

Bather with Towel 1938
Aquatint and etching
BAT
Baer 663 A.b; Bloch 287

Two Bathers 1939
Burin; BAT
Baer 668 A; Bloch 320

The Pipers 1946 (6) 1946
(illus. cat. 20.1–3)
Etching with scraper and
drypoint on zinc
Edition: 2, no. 1; Baer 731 I
Edition: 2, no. 1; Baer 731 II
Edition: 1; Baer 731 III
Edition: 2, no. 1; Baer 731 IV
Edition: 1; Baer 731 V
Edition: 2, no. 1 printed in green
Baer 731 VI
Baer 731 I–VI; Bloch 1347–49

**Illustration: Woman with
a Scarf** 1947
Sugar-lift aquatint
41 etchings; Illustration to
"Góngora: Vingt Poëmes"
Baer 753 II.B.c.2; Bloch 491

The Hen 1952
Sugar-lift aquatint, drypoint
and scraper
BAT
Baer 896 VI.B.a; Bloch 694

THE ART OF THE BULLFIGHT
[*LA TAUROMAQUIA*]
(illus. cats. 38.1–38.2)
By José Delgado, alias Pepe Illo
Published by Gustavo Gili,
Barcelona, 1959
Book of 26 sugar-lift aquatints,
printed by Lacourière-Frélaut,
Paris
Edition: 263, no.16 on Guarro
wove paper, with bull's head
watermark
[Includes supplementary edition
of 26 sugar-lift aquatints on Japan
wove paper, with no watermark;
Baer cat. 971–996 B.c]
Baer 971 B.d–973 B.d, 974 II.B.d,
975 B.d-996 B.d; Bloch 951–976

Etchings and aquatints, 1963–64
Published by Galerie Louise
Leiris, Paris, 1965; edition: 50, no. 9
Printed by Aldo Crommelynck
on wove paper with Richard de
Bas watermark
Signed and numbered

**Sculptor, Model and Two
Spectators** 1963
Baer 1112 B.b.1; Bloch 1118

Painter and Model. II 1963
Baer 1131 B.b.1; Bloch 1134

Painter with Bearded Model . . .
1963
Baer 1133 B.b.1; Bloch 1136

Painter and Model. IV 1963
Baer 1139 B.b.1; Bloch 1141

Painter in an Armchair, Model . . .
1963
Baer 1140 B.c.1; Bloch 1142

**Painter and Model, with a
Sculpture. I** 1964
Baer 1143 B.b.1; Bloch 1154

**Head of a Man in a Striped
Bathing Suit** 1964
Softground etching in eight
colors
Baer 1164 B.b.1; Bloch 1164

Smoker. V 1964
Baer 1176 B.b.1; Bloch 1176

Two Women. III 1965
Baer 1186 B.b.1; Bloch 1202

Couple 1965
Baer 1189 B.b.1; Bloch 1207

**Painter and Model before a
Painting** 1965
Baer 1197 B.b.1; Bloch 1215

**Painter and His Canvas, with
a Model** 1965
Baer 1200 B.b.1; Bloch 1218

2. LINOCUTS,
according to Baer
Published by Galerie Louise
Leiris 1960
Edition: 50, no.14
Printed by Hidalgo Arnéra on
Arches wove paper
Signed and numbered

**"Portrait of a Young Woman"
(after Cranach). II** 1958
(illus. cat. 42)
Edition: 50, no. 3
Baer 1053 III.C.a; Bloch 859

The Banderillero
(illus. cat. 43)
Baer 1225 IV.B.a; Bloch 940

Picador and Bull
(illus. cat. 44)
Baer 1226 II.B.a; Bloch 909

Picador and Bull
(illus. cat. 45)
Baer 1229 IV.B.a; Bloch 907

**Dawn Serenade, with Sleeping
Woman**
Baer 1234 II.B.a; Bloch 916

**Picador Standing with His
Horse**
Baer 1237 B.a; Bloch 912

**Picador Standing with His
Horse and a Woman**
Baer 1238 B.a; Bloch 913

**Portrait of Jacqueline Leaning
on Her Elbows** (illus. cat. 46)
Baer 1240 B.a; Bloch 922

The Grape Gatherers
Baer 1241 V.B.a; Bloch 937

The Lance. III
Baer 1243 III.B.a; Bloch 920

Head of a Woman in Profile
Baer 1246 IV.B.a; Bloch 905

Two Women Awakening
Baer 1249 II.B.a; Bloch 925

**The Morning. Two Women
Awakening**
Baer 1252 II.B.a; Bloch 924

Bacchanal
Baer 1255 B.a; Bloch 927

Night Dance with Owl
Baer 1256 II.B.a; Bloch 936

**Bacchanal with Young Goat
and Onlooker**
(illus. cover; cat. 47)
Baer 1260 III.B.f.2.α; Bloch 931

Bacchanal with Bull
Baer 1262 B.b.2.α; Bloch 932

Bacchanal with Owl
(illus. cat. 48)
Baer 1265 B.a; Bloch 938

Published by Galerie Louise
Leiris 1963
Edition: 50, no. 44
Printed by Hidalgo Arnéra
Signed and numbered

**Variation on Manet's "Déjeuner
sur l'herbe"** (illus. cat. 49)
Edition: 50, no. 29
Baer 1277 I.B.a; Bloch 1023

Head of Faun (illus. cat. 50)
Baer 1291 VI.B.b.2.α; Bloch 1094

**Large Head of a Woman in
a Hat** (illus. cat. 51)
Baer 1293 IV.B.a; Bloch 1078

Jacqueline with Headband. III
Baer 1297 III.B.b.1; Bloch 1079

**Portrait of Jacqueline in a
Flowered Hat**
Baer 1304 I.A.b.1; Bloch 1076

**Young Man Crowned with
Leaves**
Baer 1307 III.B.a; Bloch 1087

**Bearded Man Crowned with
Vine Leaves**
Baer 1308 V.B.a; Bloch 1088

**Still Life with Glass under
the Lamp** (illus. cat. 52)
Edition: 50, no. 15
Baer 1312 V.B.a; Bloch 1101

The Glass under the Lamp
Baer 1314 II.B.2.a; Bloch 1103

**Large Head of Jacqueline
with Hat**
Baer 1317 II.B.b.1; Bloch 1077

Portrait of Woman in Hat . . .
Edition: 50, no. 25, signed and
numbered
Baer 1318 V.B.a; Bloch 1072

**Portrait of Jacqueline with a
Flowery Straw Hat**
Baer 1322 II.B.a; Bloch 1075

**Portrait of Jacqueline as
Carmen**
Baer 1324 IV.B.a; Bloch 1095

"Déjeuner sur l'herbe" (after
Manet). II 1962
Baer 1329 IV.B.a; Bloch 1097

3. *SUITE 347,*
intaglio prints 1968,
according to Baer

Published by Galerie Louise
Leiris, Paris, 1969
Suite of 347 aquatints and
etchings, with combinations
of drypoint and scraper
Printed by Aldo and Piero
Crommelynck
Edition: 50, no. 44
Signed and numbered

Leiris 1 March 16–22, 1968
(illus. cat. 53.1)
Baer 1496 VII.B.b.1; Bloch 1481
Leiris 2 March 16, 1968
Baer 1497 B.b.1; Bloch 1482
Leiris 3 March 22, 1968
Baer 1498 B.b.1; Bloch 1483
Leiris 4 March 22, 1968
Baer 1499 B.b.1; Bloch 1484
Leiris 5 March 24, 1968
Baer 1500 B.b.1; Bloch 1485
Leiris 6 March 24, 1968
Baer 1501 B.b.; Bloch 1486
Leiris 7 March 24, 1968
Baer 1502 B.b.1; Bloch 1487
Leiris 8 March 25, 1968
(illus. cat. 53.2)
Baer 1503 B.b.1; Bloch 1488
Leiris 9 March 26, 1968
(illus. cat. 53.3)
Baer 1504 B.b.1; Bloch 1489
Leiris 10 March 29, 1968
Baer 1506 II.B.b.1; Bloch 1490
Leiris 11 March 29, 1968
Baer 1507 B.b.1; Bloch 1491

Leiris 13 March 30, 1968
Baer 1509 B.b.1; Bloch 1493
Leiris 14 March 30, 1968
Baer 1510 B.b.1; Bloch 1494
Leiris 15 April 1, 1968
Baer 1511 B.b.1; Bloch 1495
Leiris 16 April 3, 1968
Baer 1512 B.b.1; Bloch 1496
Leiris 17 April 6, 1968
Baer 1513 B.b.1; Bloch 1497
Leiris 18 April 6, 1968
Baer 1514 II.B.b.1; Bloch 1498
Leiris 19 April 6, 1968
Baer 1515 II.B.b.1; Bloch 1499
Leiris 20 April 8, 1968
Baer 1516 B.b.1; Bloch 1500
Leiris 21 April 8, 1968
Baer 1517 B.b.1; Bloch 1501
Leiris 22 April 8, 1968
Baer 1518 B.b.1; Bloch 1502
Leiris 23 April 8, 1968
Baer 1519 B.b.1; Bloch 1503
Leiris 24 April 11, 1968
(illus. cat. 53.4)
Baer 1520 B.b.1; Bloch 1504
Leiris 25 April 11, 1968
Baer 1521 B.b.1; Bloch 1505

Leiris 29 April 11, 1968
Baer 1525 B.b.1; Bloch 1509
Leiris 30 April 11, 1968
Baer 1526 B.b.1; Bloch 1510
Leiris 31 April 12, 1968
Baer 1527 II.B.b.1; Bloch 1511
Leiris 32 April 12, 1968
Baer 1528 B.b.1; Bloch 1512
Leiris 33 April 13, 1968
Baer 1529 B.b.1; Bloch 1513
Leiris 34 April 13, 1968
(illus. cat. 53.5)
Baer 1530 B.b.1; Bloch 1514
Leiris 35 April 13, 1968
Baer 1531 B.b.1; Bloch 1515
Leiris 36 April 13, 1968
Baer 1532 B.b.1; Bloch 1516

Leiris 37 April 13, 1968
Baer 1533 B.b.1; Bloch 1517
Leiris 38 April 14, 1968
Baer 1534 B.b.1; Bloch 1518
Leiris 39 April 15, 1968
Baer 1535 B.b.1; Bloch 1519
Leiris 40 April 15, 17–19, 1968
(illus. cat. 53.6)
Baer 1536 II.B.b.1; Bloch 1520
Leiris 41 April 15, 17–19, 1968
Baer 1537 II.B.b.1; Bloch 1521
Leiris 42 April 19, 1968
(illus. cat. 53.7)
Baer 1538 B.b.1; Bloch 1522
Leiris 43 April 20, 1968
Baer 1539 B.b.1; Bloch 1523
Leiris 44 April 20, 1968
Baer 1540 B.b.1; Bloch 1524
Leiris 45 April 21, 22, 1968
Baer 1541 II.B.b.1; Bloch 1525
Leiris 46 April 21, 1968
(illus. cat. 53.8)
Baer 1542 B.b.1; Bloch 1526
Leiris 47 April 22, 1968
Baer 1543 B.b.1; Bloch 1527
Leiris 48 April 23, 1968
(illus. cat. 53.9)
Baer 1544 B.b.1; Bloch 1528

Leiris 51 April 24, 1968
Baer 1547 II.B.b.1; Bloch 1531
Leiris 52 April 26, 1968
Baer 1548 B.b.1; Bloch 1532
Leiris 53 April 26, 1968
Baer 1549 B.b.1; Bloch 1533
Leiris 54 April 26, 1968
Baer 1550 B.b.1; Bloch 1534
Leiris 55 April 27, 28, 1968
Baer 1551 B.b.1; Bloch 1535
Leiris 56 April 28, 1968
(illus. cat. 53.9)
Baer 1552 B.b.1; Bloch 1536
Leiris 57 April 29, 1968
Baer 1553 B.b.1; Bloch 1537
Leiris 58 April 29, 1968
Baer 1554 B.b.1; Bloch 1538
Leiris 59 April 30, 1968
Baer 1555 B.b.1; Bloch 1539

Leiris 64 May 5, 6, 7, 9, 1968
(illus. cat. 53.10)
Baer 1560 V.B.b.1; Bloch 1544
Leiris 65 May 5, 1968
Baer 1561 B.b.1; Bloch 1545

Leiris 67 May 7, 1968
Baer 1563 B.b.1; Bloch 1548

Leiris 69 May 8, 1968
Baer 1565 B.b.1; Bloch 1549
Leiris 70 May 8, 1968
Baer 1566 B.b.1; Bloch 1550
Leiris 71 May 10, 1968
Baer 1567 B.b.1; Bloch 1551

Leiris 73 May 10, 1968
Baer 1569 B.b.1; Bloch 1553
Leiris 74 May 11, 1968
(illus. cat. 53.11)
Baer 1570 B.b.1; Bloch 1554

Leiris 80 May 12, 1968
Baer 1576 B.b.1; Bloch 1560
Leiris 81 May 13, 1968
(illus. cat. 53.12)
Baer 1577 B.b.1; Bloch 1561
Leiris 82 May 13, 1968
Baer 1578 B.b.1; Bloch 1562

Leiris 85 May 14, 1968
(illus. cat. 53.13)
Baer 1581 B.b.1; Bloch 1565

Leiris 87 May 15, 1968
(illus. cat. 53.14)
Baer 1583 III B.b.1; Bloch 1567

Leiris 97 May 16, 1968
Baer 1593 VI.B.b.1; Bloch 1577
Leiris 98 May 17, 1968
Baer 1594 B.b.1; Bloch 1578
Leiris 99 May 18, 1968
(illus. cat. 53.15)
Baer 1595 B.b.1; Bloch 1579
Leiris 100 May 17, 1968
Baer 1596 II.B.b.1; Bloch 1580

Leiris 104 May 21, 1968
Baer 1600 B.b.1; Bloch 1584

Leiris 109 May 25, 1968
(illus. cat. 53.16)
Baer 1605 B.b.1; Bloch 1589

Leiris 115 May 26, 1968
(illus. cat. 53.17)
Baer 1611 B.b.1; Bloch 1595

Leiris 123 May 28, 1968
(illus. cat. 53.18)
Baer 1619 B.b.1; Bloch 1604

Leiris 134 June 1, 1968
(illus. cat. 53.19)
Baer 1630 B.b.1; Bloch 1614
Leiris 135 June 1, 1968
Baer 1631 B.b.1; Bloch 1615

Leiris 142 June 4, 1968
(illus. cat. 53.20)
Baer 1638 IV.B.b.1; Bloch 1622
Leiris 143 June 7, 1968
Baer 1639 B.b.1; Bloch 1623
Leiris 144 June 7, 1968
Baer 1640 B.b.1; Bloch 1624

Leiris 153 June 10, 1968
Baer 1649 B.b.1; Bloch 1633

Leiris 159 June 15, 1968
Baer 1655 B.b.1; Bloch 1639
Leiris 160 June 15, 1968
Baer 1656 B.b.1; Bloch 1640
Leiris 161 June 15, 1968
(illus. cat. 53.21)
Baer 1657 B.b.1; Bloch 1641

Leiris 180 June 22, 1968
Baer 1676 III.B.b.1; Bloch 1660

Leiris 186 June 25, 1968
Baer 1682 B.b.1; Bloch 1666
Leiris 187 June 25 and July 17, 1968
Baer 1683 B.b.1; Bloch 1667

Leiris 196 June 30, 1968
(illus. cat. 53.22)
Baer 1692 III.B.b.1; Bloch 1676
Leiris 197 June 30, 1968
Baer 1693 II.B.b.1; Bloch 1677

Leiris 201 July 5, 1968
Baer 1697 III.B.b.1; Bloch 1681

Leiris 204 July 15, 1968
Baer 1700 B.b.1; Bloch 1684
Leiris 205 July15, 1968
Baer 1701 B.b.1; Bloch 1685
Leiris 206 July 16, 1968
(illus. cat. 53.23)
Baer 1702 B.b.1; Bloch 1686

Leiris 217 July 26, 1968
Baer 1713 B.b.1; Bloch 1697

Leiris 221 July 27, 1968
Baer 1717 B.b.1; Bloch 1701
Leiris 222 July 27, 1968
Baer 1718 B.b.1; Bloch 1702
Leiris 223 July 28, 1968
(illus. cat. 53.24)
Baer 1719 II.B.b.1; Bloch 1703

Leiris 232 August 2, 1968
Baer 1729 II.B.b.1; Bloch 1713

Leiris 251 August 5, 1968
Baer 1748 B.b.1; Bloch 1731

Leiris 277 August 14, 1968
Baer 1774 B.b.1; Bloch 1756

Leiris 281 August 15, 1968
Baer 1778 B.b.1; Bloch 1761

Leiris 285 August 18, 1968
Baer 1782 B.b.1; Bloch 1765

Leiris 288 August 19, 1968
Baer 1785 B.b.1; Bloch 1768
Leiris 289 August 20, 1968
Baer 1786 B.b.1; Bloch 1769

Leiris 291 August 22, 1968
Baer 1788 B.b.1; Bloch 1771
Leiris 292 August 23, 1968
Baer 1789 B.b.1; Bloch 1772
Leiris 293 August 23, 1968
Baer 1790 B.b.1; Bloch 1773

Leiris 296 August 29, 1968
Baer 1793 B.b.1; Bloch 1776

Leiris 299 August 31, 1968
(illus. cat. 53.25)
Baer 1796 B.b.1; Bloch 1779

Leiris 300 August 31, 1968
Baer 1797 B.b.1; Bloch 1780

Leiris 302 September 1, 1968
Baer 1799 B.b.1; Bloch 1782

4. LITHOGRAPHS,
by Mourlot number

Interior Scene 1926
Not printed by Mourlot
Mourlot XXI; Bloch 74

Woman's Head (2) 1945
BAT; 1 of 18 ARP
Mourlot 1; Bloch 375

Woman's Head on Black
Background (2) 1945
BAT; 1 of 18 ARP
Mourlot 2; Bloch 376

(Stylized) Woman's Head on
Black Background (2) 1945
BAT; 1 of 18 ARP
Mourlot 3; Bloch 377

Woman's Head (3) 1945
1 of 18 ARP, i; BAT, ii; 1 of 18
ARP, ii
Mourlot 4; Bloch 384

Head of Young Girl (5) 1945
1 of 18 ARP, i–iv; BAT, iv
Mourlot 5; Bloch 383

Still Life with Fruit Stand (6) 1945
3 of 3 Trial proofs, i (3); 1 of 18
ARP, ii, iii; edition: 50, no. 49, iii
Mourlot 6; Bloch 379

Head of Young Girl (4) 1945
Unique impression before i;
1 of 18 ARP, i–iii
Mourlot 7; not in Bloch

Head of Young Boy (3) 1945
1 of 18 ARP, unpublished, i, iii;
unrecorded working proof
between ii and iii
Mourlot 8; Bloch 378

Head of Young Girl (20) 1945
1 of 2 Trial proofs, i; unique trial
proof, ii; 1 of 18 ARP, ii–x;
BAT, x; i, ii (2), iv (2), viii, ix, x
Mourlot 9; Bloch 393

Two Small Bulls 1945
1 of 18 ARP
Mourlot 10; Bloch 1342

Long-Haired Young Girl (8)
1945
2 of 2 Trial proofs, i (2); BAT, vi;
1 of 18 ARP, ii–vi
Mourlot 12; Bloch 380

Arabesque 1945
1 of 18 ARP
Mourlot 15; not in Bloch

Two Nude Women (9) 1946
(illus. cats. 14.1–14.4)
Unrecorded proof between vii
and viii;
Intermediate proof between vii
and viii;
Unique impression, viii; trial
proofs, viii, xi, xii, xiv (2), xv
Mourlot 16; Bloch 390

The Bull (12) 1945
(illus. cats. 15.1–15.6)
1 of 18 ARP, i–vi, viii, ix;
working proof between i and ii;
Trial proofs, vii, x, xi
Mourlot 17; Bloch 389

Pages of Sketches . . . 1945
1 of 18 ARP
Mourlot 18; Bloch 381

Heads of Rams (2) 1945
1 of 18 ARP; proof
Mourlot 19; Bloch 382

Still Life with Vase of Flowers
1945
Unique impression
Mourlot 20; not in Bloch

Bulls, Rams, and Birds 1945
(illus. cat. 16)
1 of 18 ARP
Mourlot 21; Bloch 1344

Three Birds 1945
1 of 18 ARP
Mourlot 22; not in Bloch

Birds in Flight 1945
1 of 18 ARP
Mourlot 23; not in Bloch

The Circus (3) 1945
1 of 18 ARP, i, ii; BAT, ii
Mourlot 24; Bloch 385

Bullfight under a Black Sun (2)
1946 (illus. cat. 17)
BAT; proof
Mourlot 25; Bloch 1346

Bullfight (2) 1946
BAT; 1 of 18 ARP
Mourlot 26; Bloch 387

Side View of Bull 1945
(illus. cat. 18)
1 of 18 ARP
Mourlot 27; not in Bloch

Eight Silhouettes (2) 1946
(illus. cat. 19)
BAT; 1 of 18 ARP
Mourlot 29; Bloch 388

Still Life with Three Apples 1945
1 of 18 ARP
Mourlot 30; not in Bloch

Still Life with Three Apples (3)
1945
1 of 2 impressions in black;
1 of 2 trial proofs;
Unrecorded variation or variant
Mourlot 31; not in Bloch

Still Life with Three Apples
1945
Mourlot 31[related]; not in Bloch

Composition (3) 1946
1 of 18 ARP, i–iii
Mourlot 32; Bloch 391

Composition with Glass and
Apple (6) 1946
1 of 18 ARP, i (2), ii (2), iii (2)
Mourlot 33; Bloch 392

Shells and Birds (5) 1946
1 of 18 ARP, i (2), ii (2); BAT, ii
Mourlot 34; Bloch 394

Black Pitcher and Death's Head
1946
BAT
Mourlot 35; Bloch 395

Composition with Skull 1946
1 of 6 ARP
Mourlot 36; not in Bloch

Studies (3) 1946
1 of 2 trial proofs of the 1st–3rd
stones
Mourlot 37; not in Bloch

Françoise (4) 1946
BAT (4)
Mourlot 43–46; Bloch 399–402

Two Turtle-Doves, I 1946
BAT
Mourlot 49; Bloch 405

Owl with White Background
1947
BAT (dedicated to Mourlot)
Mourlot 53; Bloch 408

Owl in Crayon 1947
BAT (dedicated to Mourlot)
Mourlot 57; Bloch 412

Fauns and the She-Centaur 1947
BAT (dedicated to Mourlot)
Mourlot 59; Bloch 413

Ines and Her Child (2) 1947
BAT (2)
Mourlot 60 and 61; Bloch 414
and 415

Pigeon on Gray Background 1947
(illus. cat. 21)
BAT
Mourlot 64; Bloch 418

White Pigeon on Black
Background 1947
BAT
Mourlot 65; Bloch 420

Fat Pigeon 1947
BAT
Mourlot 66; Bloch 419

Bust of a Young Girl 1947
BAT
Mourlot 67; Bloch 421

Head of a Young Girl 1947
BAT, iv
Mourlot 68; Bloch 423

Portrait of Gongora 1947
BAT
Mourlot 70; Bloch 424

Young Pigeon in Its Nest 1947
BAT
Mourlot 71; Bloch 427

Pigeon and Its Little Ones 1947
BAT
Mourlot 72; Bloch 433

Composition with Vase of
Flowers 1947
(illus. cat. 22)
BAT
Mourlot 74; Bloch 426

Woman with a Necklace 1947
BAT
Mourlot 84; Bloch 438

Large Profile 1947
BAT
Mourlot 85; Bloch 444

Still Life with Stoneware Pot
1947
BAT
Mourlot 86; Bloch 443

Seated Nude in Profile 1947
BAT
Mourlot 103; Bloch 454

Seated Woman and Sleeping
Woman 1947
BAT
Mourlot 104; Bloch 455

Head of Young Woman 1947
BAT
Mourlot 106; Bloch 458

Vase of Flowers with Floral
Carpet 1947
BAT
Mourlot 107; Bloch 459

August 8th 1947 Composition
1947
BAT
Mourlot 108; Bloch 460

"David and Bathsheba"
(after Cranach) (5) 1947
(illus. cats. 23.1–23.3)
BAT, i, ii; ed.: 50, no. 19, ii; ed.:
50, no. 29, i; ed.: 50, no. 5, iv
Mourlot 109; Bloch 439 (i), 440
(ii), 441 (iv)

"David and Bathsheba"
(after Cranach) (2) 1947
(illus. cat. 24)
BAT, i (dedicated to Fernand
Mourlot); ed.: 50, no. 30, i
Mourlot 109A; Bloch 442

Pan 1948
BAT
Mourlot 111; Bloch 518

Faun with Branches 1948
BAT
Mourlot 113; Bloch 520

Musician Faun No. 3–5 (3) 1948
BAT (3)
Mourlot 114–116;
Bloch 521–523

The Song of the Dead
1945
Book with five double sheets
with text and one proof sheet
Pp. 21–29, 37–40, 65–68, 89–92
Mourlot 117; Bloch 524

First-Third Vallauris Posters (3)
1948
BAT (3)
Mourlot 118B, 119B, 120B;
Bloch 526, 528, 530

Head of Woman 1948
BAT
Mourlot 122; not in Bloch

The Studio 1948
BAT
Mourlot 125; Bloch 576

Composition 1948
(illus. cat. 25)
BAT
Mourlot 127; Bloch 578

Figure (3) 1948
BAT (3)
Mourlot 128–130; Bloch 579,
580; not in Bloch

Woman in an Armchair, No. 4
1949 (illus. cat. 26)
Edition: 50, no. 38, v
Mourlot 137; Bloch 588

The Dove (2) 1949
(illus. cat. 27)
BAT (dedicated to Mourlot);
edition: 50, no. 41
Mourlot 141; Bloch 583

The Lobster 1949
(illus. cat. 28)
BAT
Mourlot 143; Bloch 584

The Toad 1949
(illus. cat. 29)
BAT
Mourlot 144; Bloch 585

Head of a Young Girl 1949
BAT, ii
Mourlot 149; Bloch 589

The Young Artist 1949
BAT, ii
Mourlot 150; Bloch 609

White Bust on Black 1949
BAT
Mourlot 161; Bloch 592

Figure 1949
BAT
Mourlot 162; Bloch 593

The Bull's Return 1945
BAT
Mourlot 167; Bloch 386

The Great Bullfight 1949
BAT, i
Mourlot 168; Bloch 598

Bullfight, the Picador 1949
BAT
Mourlot 172; Bloch 599

The Checkered Blouse
1949
(illus. cat. 30)
BAT (dedicated to Mourlot)
Mourlot 175A; Bloch 601

Woman with Hairnet 1956
(illus. cat. 37)
BAT, iv
Mourlot 178A; Bloch 612

"Venus and Cupid" (after
Cranach) 1949
BAT, ii
Mourlot 183; Bloch 613

Youth 1950
Edition: 50, no. 30, ii
Mourlot 188; Bloch 675

Flowers in a Vase 1950
BAT (dedicated to Fernand
Mourlot)
Mourlot 189; Bloch 674

Dove in Flight, Black
Background 1950
BAT
Mourlot 190; Bloch 676

Flying Dove 1950
BAT
Mourlot 191; Bloch 677

Flight of the Dove 1950
BAT
Mourlot 192; Bloch 678

Dove in Flight 1950
BAT (dedicated to Mourlot)
Mourlot 193; Bloch 679

Françoise against a Gray
Background (2) 1950
(illus. cat. 31)
Proof i; BAT, ii
Mourlot 195; Bloch 681

The Pike 1950
BAT
Mourlot 196; Bloch 683

The Departure 1951
BAT, x
Mourlot 201; Bloch 686

Don Quixote and Sancho
Panza. I/II (2) 1951
BAT (2)
Mourlot 207–208;
Bloch 688–689

Bound Hands. I–IV (4)
1952
BAT (4)
Mourlot 210–213;
Bloch 708–711

Balzac (3) 1952
BAT (3)
Mourlot 225–227;
Bloch 723–725

Paloma and Her Doll . . . (2)
1952
BAT; edition 50: no. 36
Mourlot 228–229;
Bloch 726–727

Paloma 1952
BAT
Mourlot 230; Bloch 728

The Embroidered Sweater
1953
BAT
Mourlot 231; Bloch 729

Woman's Head, Three-Quarter
View 1953
BAT
Mourlot 232; Bloch 730

Head with Chignon
1953
BAT
Mourlot 233; Bloch 731

Still Life with Book 1953
BAT
Mourlot 234; Bloch 732

The Family 1953
BAT
Mourlot 235; Bloch 738

Gardens at Vallauris 1953
BAT
Mourlot 236; Bloch 733

Landscape at Vallauris 1953
BAT
Mourlot 237; Bloch 734

"The Italian Woman" (after
Orsel) (3) 1953
(illus. cat. 32.)
1 of 5 ARP, i; BAT, ii; proof, ii
Mourlot 238; Bloch 740

Mother and Children . . . 1953
BAT
Mourlot 239; Bloch 739

Games and Reading 1953
(illus. cat. 33)
BAT
Mourlot 240; Bloch 741

Head on Black Background (3)
1953
BAT (2); proof (1)
Mourlot 241; Bloch 742

Woman with Monkey 1954
BAT
Mourlot 243; Bloch 747

Reclining Model 1954
BAT
Mourlot 244; Bloch 749

Dances 1954
BAT
Mourlot 246; Bloch 750

Bull at Play 1954
BAT
Mourlot 247; Bloch 751

Dance of the Banderillas 1954
(illus. cat. 34)
BAT
Mourlot 248; Bloch 752

Three Women and the
Toreador 1954
BAT
Mourlot 251; Bloch 755

Rehearsal 1954
BAT
Mourlot 252; Bloch 756

Nude Pose 1954
BAT
Mourlot 255; Bloch 761

Two Nude Models 1954
BAT
Mourlot 256; Bloch 762

Model and Two Figures 1954
BAT
Mourlot 258; Bloch 759

Old Painter's Studio 1954
BAT
Mourlot 260; Bloch 760

Nude with Chair 1954
BAT
Mourlot 261; Bloch 763

Painter and His Model 1954
BAT
Mourlot 262; Bloch 765

Little Artist 1956
BAT
Mourlot 263; Bloch 768

Two Clowns 1954
BAT
Mourlot 264; Bloch 766

"Women of Algiers . . ."
(after Delacroix). I
1955 (illus. cat. 35)
1 of 5 ARP, 1st variation
Mourlot 265; not in Bloch

"Women of Algiers . . ."
(after Delacroix). II (4)
1955 (illus. cats. 36.1–36.2)
1 of 5 ARP, 2nd variation,
i, ii, iii, iv
Mourlot 266; not in Bloch

Cover for a Catalogue 1956
BAT
Mourlot 268; Bloch 792

In Picasso's Studio 1955
BAT
Mourlot 269; Bloch 779

Portrait of a Woman. II
1955
BAT
Mourlot 272; Bloch 780

Two Squatting Women
1956
BAT
Mourlot 274; Bloch 790

Squatting Woman with
Raised Arm 1956
BAT
Mourlot 275; Bloch 791

Wounded Toreador 1956
BAT
Mourlot 276; Bloch 799

Reclining Man and
Squatting Woman 1956
BAT
Mourlot 277; Bloch 797

Bacchanal 1956
BAT
Mourlot 280; Bloch 795

Owl, Glass and Flower 1956
BAT, ii
Mourlot 282; Bloch 1272

Antique Scene 1956
BAT
Mourlot 286; Bloch 801

Three-Color Profile 1956
BAT
Mourlot 288; Bloch 826

Collection of Small Pictures
1956
BAT
Mourlot 290; Bloch 828

Fauns Dance (2) 1957
BAT (2)
Mourlot 291; Bloch 830

Bacchanal 1957
BAT
Mourlot 292; Bloch 831

Bullfighting Game 1957
BAT
Mourlot 293; Bloch 832

Jacqueline in Profile 1957
BAT
Mourlot 294; Bloch 833

Portrait of Kahnweiler. I–III (3)
1957 (illus. cat. 39)
BAT (3)
Mourlot 295–297;
Bloch 834–836

Poster for the 1957 Exhibition
1957
BAT
Mourlot 299; Bloch 1275

Composition 1957
BAT
Mourlot 300; Bloch 838

Poster for the Ceret Museum
1957
BAT
Mourlot 301; Bloch 1278

Bullfight 1957
BAT
Mourlot 303; Bloch 840

Horsewoman and Clowns 1961
BAT
Mourlot 304; Bloch 844

Vase with Flowers 1961
BAT
Mourlot 305; Bloch 841

Bust in Profile (2) 1957
(illus. cat. 40)
BAT, i, iii
Mourlot 306; Bloch 845

Woman with Flowered Blouse
1958 (illus. cat. 41)
BAT, iii
Mourlot 307; Bloch 847

Bust with Checkered Blouse (2)
1957
BAT, i, ii
Mourlot 308; Bloch 849

Jacqueline Reading (2) 1957
BAT, i, iii
Mourlot 309; Bloch 851– 852

Woman with Chignon 1957
BAT, i
Mourlot 310; Bloch 853

Portrait of Jacqueline,
Right Profile 1958
BAT, iii
Mourlot 310; Bloch 853

Bust of Woman with
White Bodice 1957
BAT, i, iii
Mourlot 311; Bloch 848

Jacqueline with Black
Kerchief 1958
BAT, ii
Mourlot 316; Bloch 873

Old King 1959
BAT
Mourlot 317; Bloch 869

Bullfighter and Woman
1960
BAT
Mourlot 332; Bloch 1005

Horsewoman 1960
BAT
Mourlot 333; Bloch 999

Homage to Bacchus 1960
BAT
Mourlot 336; Bloch 1006

Portrait of Arthur Rimbaud
1960
BAT
Mourlot 342; Bloch 1007

Bullfight 1961
BAT
Mourlot 344; Bloch 1011

Bulls and Bullfighters 1961
BAT
Mourlot 345; Bloch 1012

Flowers (for U.C.L.A.) 1961
Edition: 100, no. 45
Mourlot 351; Bloch 1297

Picnic 1962
BAT
Mourlot 352; Bloch 1024

Football 1961
BAT
Mourlot 356; Bloch 1019

Family Portrait. I (2) 1962
BAT; BAT, unique, related proof
Mourlot 383; Bloch 1029

Family Portrait. III 1962
BAT
Mourlot 385; Bloch 1031

Family Portrait. IV (2) 1962
BAT; edition: 50, no. 9
Mourlot 386; Bloch 1033

Family Portrait, V (2) 1962
BAT; edition: 50, no. 9
Mourlot 387; Bloch 1032

Joys of the Night 1959
Edition: 2000, no. 363
Not in Mourlot; not in Bloch